MW00611529

HUNTING CHUKAR

*A No-Nonsense Guide to the Successful Pursuit
Of The West's Most Elusive Game Bird*

By

RICHARD O'TOOLE

HUNTING CHUKAR

*A No-Nonsense Guide to the Successful Pursuit
Of The West's Most Elusive Game Bird*

By

RICHARD O'TOOLE

Copyright 2003 by Richard O'Toole

Published in The United States of America

ISBN 1-931291-29-2

Library of Congress Control Number 2003104678

First Edition

ALL RIGHTS RESERVED

No part of this publication may be reproduced, stored in a retrieval system, or transmitted in any form or by any means without the prior written permission of the copyright owner or the publisher.

STONEYDALE PRESS PUBLISHING COMPANY
523 Main Street • P.O. Box 188
Stevensville, Montana 59870
Phone: 406-777-2729

DEDICATION

To:

Roger Hutchings
Justin O'Toole
Rick Schaefer
Bill Young
Fine outdoorsmen, superb companions

ACKNOWLEDGMENTS

I want to thank those stalwart friends who so kindly an productively reviewed this manuscript: Len and Jo Braarud, Roge Hutchings, John LaCroix, Sharon Schaefer and Phil Simonski.

Thanks also to my wife, Mary Ellen, and the Plush Huntin Widows Society for permission to reproduce some of their exceller chukar recipes.

Finally, I am infinitely grateful to the expert Oregonian chuka hunters interviewed for this book: John Crafton, Redmon Howard Davol, Ashland; William Ellis, Bend; Gaynor Goth, Gran Pass; Bob Hearth, Medford; Steve Leonard, Prineville; Dav Marsh, Bend; Phil Simonski, Baker City; and John Sulliva Redmond. Meeting these hunters and discussing their varie hunting experiences was a highlight of my year.

Table of Contents

FOREWORD

I was more than a little irritated when Rick O'Toole wanted to climb "just one more hill" to look for chukar, after asking another rhetorical question about this phantom bird...

"If you are that curious about chukar behavior, why not get serious, do some research and write the book?" was my reply. Rick's response to that challenge is the book you hold before you. It is the most comprehensive discussion yet written about this bird and provides clear and detailed methods for hunting chukar which will both interest you and improve your hunting results.

Rick is well suited to the task of characterizing the behavior of this game bird. He spent thirty years as a physician specializing in the esoteric field of infectious diseases. The study of microbes has much in common with the study of chukar: both are sometimes difficult to detect. He brings the same curiosity and intellect to the subject of chukar hunting that he so successfully applied to complex medical problems.

But Rick is no "armchair expert", as the practical pointers given in the following text will attest. He spent every spare minute for the past forty years hunting and fishing, primarily in the Pacific Northwest. He has walked hundreds of miles of chukar country and has driven hundreds more to interview experienced upland game bird hunters. You will learn more about chukar hunting by reading this book than by hiking rimrock country with a hope and a dream. I know I did.

Richard A. Schaefer
Fellow hunter of the phantom chukar.

INTRODUCTION

Despite the fact that no relative of mine was ever known to ave held a rifle or shotgun; I was clearly born with the hunting ene. As a kid, I loved target shooting with a .22 rifle while doing me in summer camps. I obtained one of my own, a Remington ingle shot, at twelve, and somehow did no permanent harm with in the neighborhood. At fourteen, I moved up to a Fox 12 gauge ouble barreled shotgun with which I harassed dove in Oklahoma, nen pheasant in Wisconsin and diving ducks along the frozen nores of Lake Michigan.

At college in Western Massachusetts, I learned to hunt ruffed rouse without a dog. In the Army, I hunted bobwhite quail in outh Carolina and puddle ducks in the rice fields along the Edisto iver.

Medical School in New York City brought hunting to a mporary halt, but the next eight years in Seattle provided the pportunity to hunt upland game birds in Eastern Washington and aterfowl off the mouth of the Skagit River.

My wife, three children and I moved to Medford in the Rogue alley of southeastern Oregon in 1971 where I practiced Internal ledicine until I retired in 1997. Oregon has proven to be a onderful environment for working, raising a family...and hunting. ve pursued all manner of birds during these years and have come o enjoy hunting chukar most of all. My reasons for this preference are pretty straightforward: chukar are reasonably abundant in thos western states having hunting seasons, and they are found primaril on Public Lands. The only special equipment required for huntin them is a dog; therefore, it isn't an expensive sport. They ar challenging birds to find and to shoot, their flavor is excellent, an in pursuing them, one may also encounter Valley Quail an Hungarian Partridge. What more could you ask?

My chukar education began thirty years ago. It originall consisted of little more than random magazine articles, fiel experiences and anecdotal conversations with hunting acquaint ances. When hunting, I went out of my way to talk to every hunte I encountered; of course, there weren't very many of them since major objective in hunting chukar is the avoidance of other hunter: Subsequently, I turned to the literature of the Wildlife Biologist i order to gain a better understanding of the bird's history an behavior. In the course of constructing this book, I contacted th Departments of Fish and Wildlife in each state which conducted hunting season for chukar in 1998 or 1999. California, Nevada an Washington provided the most complete data and indicated tha chukar hunters in those states harvested an average of less than tw birds per hunter for each day hunted (1-3). These low number: reflecting relatively poor hunter success, further stimulated m desire to provide helpful guidance to my fellow hunters.

Finally, through personal contacts and referrals, I located th experienced hunters discussed in this book in order to clarif certain issues. Although most of this book refers to experiences i Oregon, I have also hunted in Nevada, California and Washingtor It is clear that the concepts put forth here are applicable to all state having huntable populations of chukar.

I hope that the information presented will help you to bette appreciate this remarkable bird, enhance your enjoyment of th hunting experience and put more birds in your bag. Also, the autho actively seeks readers' comments and criticisms. Please send thes to him at the Stoneydale Press address listed on the back cover c the book.

1

EARLY DAYS

Walt Fisher introduced me to chukar hunting in 1972. Walt was retired mink rancher from the Oregon Coast with extensive unting experience. A huge man in his mid-sixties, he possessed a narvelously dry sense of humor. He suffered from chronic ongestive heart failure which did not prevent him from enjoying is favorite activity: jump shooting mallards in a nearby marsh which he referred to as "the swamp." He was a superb wing shot, nd he wasn't shy about letting us know when he returned with nore ducks than shotshells expended.

Two of my friends and I were guests for a week at Walt's ompound in the Warner Valley in south-central Oregon, where we unted ducks and quail. After lunch one warm October day he nvited us to join him in a chukar hunt. He explained that the bird as not indigenous to North America and had been introduced by e Oregon Fish and Game Department. The chukar had achieved oderate survival success in the arid, desolate, rocky terrain that naracterized the hills around the Warner Valley. Walt described e chukar as a bird slightly smaller than the ruffed grouse and qually palatable. He noted that they hated to fly, and, when reatened, would run uphill or fly downhill.

We started out in the early afternoon of a very hot October day. 'alt drove with his friend Bob in the passenger seat, and we three erched uncomfortably on narrow benches in the canopied bed of s elderly pickup truck. We tried to track our progress by peering rough the narrow, opaque plastic window in the side of the nopy. We drove and drove and climbed and climbed narrow dirt

roads; we saw nothing but desert, rocks, sage and sun. After a
eternity, our level of excitement had begun to lose its hard edg
when the truck stopped abruptly. Walt announced that the prey ha
been sighted. We stumbled out into the blazing sunshine and sa
a formidably steep hill rising before us. Walt assured us that man
chukar had flown around the base of the hill and were walking u
the far side toward the top where they would feel secure. O
genial host explained that our best tactic for getting birds did not l
in rushing directly up the hill after them. Instead, he instructed u
to circle the base of the hill opposite the route taken by the bird
climb to the top, stay out of sight of the birds, then descend ar
confront them from above.

Accordingly, three out-of-shape, naive physicians in their la
thirties started up the hill. With muscles energized by visions of tl
brisk action awaiting us at the summit, we slipped and stumbled u
the slope, moving much too rapidly in our eagerness to beat eac
other to the top. We finally gasped our way across the crest of tl
hill where we could see birds falling from the sky far below, a
good old Walt and Bob harvested the bounty we had blocked off f
them. It had been a long, hot climb, and it was quite a while befo
our senses of humor fully recovered.

We saw no more birds that day, but we did admire the beau
of the birds, and as table fare they lived up to their billing. W
continued to hunt ducks and quail in subsequent years; howeve
chukar hunting began to occupy more of my time and intere:
Although I lived and worked in the Cascade Range of mountains
western Oregon, I found myself drawn to the high desert of easte
Oregon. This country is remote and contains vast tracts of lar
which are largely uninhabited. It is rough and unforgiving territo
which, despite its apparent barrenness, supports a remarkab
volume and variety of wildlife. The air is clean and dry, the sl
enormous and the views are endless. The terrain is characterized l
mountains and valleys with north-south axes running parallel
each other. The soil is composed of dirt, rock and sand covered l
sage and scattered juniper. There is a strong sense of the past in th
country and an unavoidable awareness of the hardiness of o
ancestors who attempted to settle this land. Among ranchers ar

ther residents of the high desert there is a prevailing respect for those who preceded them. And of greatest importance is the fact that most of this is Public Land. Very little of the privately owned land in eastern Oregon is accessible for the hunter today. This is primarily attributable to the development of leasing arrangements between a farmer or rancher and groups of individuals who pay a fee for exclusive hunting rights on his parcel of land. For the landowner, such an arrangement provides some income and also serves as a ready and understandable justification for denying access to others seeking to hunt on his property. Over the years I've knocked on dozens of doors in this area and, except for the blue heelers which often attached themselves to my ankle, I have enjoyed talking with many fine people. Regrettably, they consistently denied my request to hunt on their property.

Occasionally these encounters proved unpleasant. Ten years

Those areas of the western United States inhabited by chukar are described by some as barren and desolate. To the chukar hunter, these lands are beautiful and monumental.

ago, during the hunting season, my wife and I explored extrem
southeastern Oregon. We were attempting to follow the roug
outline of the old Oregon Trail, but we were having troubl
following it across the featureless land when we came upon th
largest collection of chukar I have ever seen. When we stopped t
admire them, an irate fellow came rushing up to us in his picku
truck. He accused us of intending to commit depredations on h
chukar which were on land that he leased, and which we wer
illegally traversing, etc., etc. Calm ensued when he realized that w
were neither on his property nor hunting. He informed us that h
lived in Nevada, but that he had leased hunting rights on this larg
ranch in Oregon for almost twenty years. During that time he ha
released ten thousand chukar for his personal sport. It was obviou
that he was using the property to run a hunting club: anoth
practice that is enjoying increasing popularity and often command
remarkable fees.

We accepted the inevitable and stopped knocking on door
Instead we took advantage of the widespread availability
beautiful, remote Public Lands. We hunted chukar in the same are
we had always used for quail and waterfowl and didn't have muc
success. We finally realized the fact that there wasn't much poi
in continuing this effort. Either there were too few birds in the are
or our hunting methods were flawed. Since the latter possibility w
unthinkable, my hunting partners and I decided to undertake a tr
to a different area and to dedicate our efforts solely to chuka
Inquiries among hunting acquaintances regarding regions of th
state abounding in chukar were greeted with predictab
amusement, but we did obtain some reliable leads.

Pursuing one of these, we found ourselves in southeaste
Oregon adjacent to the Nevada state line where we hunted f
several days. We hiked over parched, rocky hills dotted wi
abandoned as well as active gold mines, and we found chukar, lc
of chukar. We learned a few basic facts about chukar and abo
ourselves. Chukar have excellent vision, and they are wary bird
They *love* to run uphill and they are very good at it. We don't ar
we aren't.

We were unable to get within shotgun range by pursuing the

uphill, and were unable to get above them by detouring, because they were able to keep track of us on the relatively open slopes. On the third day, my friend, Bill Young, flushed an obviously retarded bird and shot it. It was the only bird harvested by three of us in four hard days of hunting. It was obvious that we didn't know how to hunt chukar. Some research into its habits and behavior was urgently needed if the results of our hunting efforts were to improve..

Rimrock, cheatgrass and water: the ingredients essential to a healthy chukar population are found here.

2

CHUKAR HISTORY/HABITAT

Initially, I reviewed the magazine and newspaper articles I had collected during the previous ten years. Then I read everything I could find in the public library and on the shelves of large bookstores. The magazine articles were brief and did not discuss chukar behavior in detail. None of the books devoted more than a chapter to chukar hunting; therefore, I returned to the public library. With the assistance of infinitely patient librarians and an excellent interlibrary loan system, I was able to access several informative publications which described the birds biologic behavior (4-10). Several of these were studies performed by game biologists in those Western States most successful in establishing healthy populations of chukar between 1953 and 1970. Their findings have been largely confirmed and extended by recent studies carried out in Idaho (11) and Oregon (12).

The chukar is a red-legged rock partridge. It belongs in the genus *Alectoris*, from the Greek *alector*, meaning cock. *Alectoris chukar* is the currently accepted designation of the Asiatic species which prevails in North America (4). Chukar are found widespread throughout the Old World: from Spain across the northern Mediterranean Sea, through Iraq and India to Tibet, Western China and Mongolia.

In hand, the chukar is a beautiful bird with distinctive markings. There is a well defined black mask that passes through the eyes, curving downward to the upper chest and which contrasts in hue with the bird's red beak and off-white cheeks and chin. Parallel dark bars are formed by the tips of adjacent flank feathers

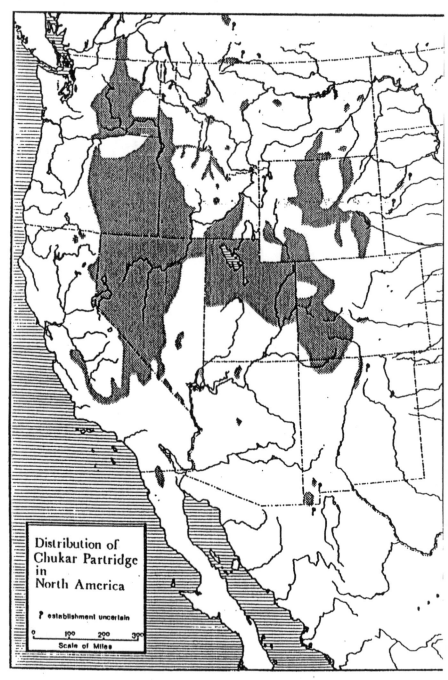

Distribution of Chukar Partridge in North America

? establishment uncertain

0   100   200   300
Scale of Miles

FIGURE 1. FROM CHRISTENSEN (4)

and contrast with adjacent whitish-tan hues. The legs and feet are red and large, and their feet have sturdy claws. They are members of the zoological order *Galliformes* (from the Latin, gallus = cock + form), birds of terrestrial habits with relatively large bodies and small wings. The large legs are well adapted for running and scratching on the ground where most of their food is found. Their average weight is somewhat more than one pound, and cocks are slightly heavier than hens. Their markings are identical; therefore, sexes cannot be distinguished in the field. In hand, biologists can identify males and females based on differences in shank length and tarsal spurs

In flight, the chukar appears to be a brown-grey bird of medium size with unexceptional markings, since it is usually fleeing the intruder and presents only tail feathers, wing and dorsal body for inspection. Occasionally when flushed, especially if the bird makes an extended effort to gain altitude, the barred flanks and red beak may be seen from the side. When downed by shot, the bird's coloring blends so well with virtually all terrain that retrieval without a dog is very difficult.

The first recorded attempt to introduce chukar to this country took place in 1893 (4). This effort failed, but, subsequently, many private individuals, states and private game clubs continued to import one or another of multiple species of *Alectoris* into the United States. Attempts to establish the chukar have been made by 42 states and six Canadian Provinces and have met with success in only eleven Western states, British Columbia and six Hawaiian Islands. The best results were obtained with birds imported from Northern India and what is now West Pakistan, where they flourished in the dry foothills of the Himalayan mountains.

These birds have unique habitat requirements. They tolerate a remarkable range of temperatures and altitudes, from sea level to 12,000 feet in this country. However, they are intolerant of moisture and are not encountered in areas with average annual rainfall in excess of 25 inches (4). They inhabit terrain composed of mountains, valleys, and steep canyons. Soil is rocky and hillsides are covered with talus, rocky outcrops and low lying brush. Scattered juniper may be present, but chukar avoid heavily wooded terrain. Given these requirements, it's no surprise that the birds are distributed unevenly within the states in which they have become established. Chukar are found primarily in Eastern Washington and Oregon, Northern and Western Nevada, Southeastern California, Northern Utah, Western Colorado, Western Idaho and in scattered regions of Wyoming, Montana, Arizona and New Mexico. (Fig. 1)

Ask a seasoned chukar hunter how he goes about finding birds and he will likely respond, "Find rimrock, cheat grass and water and you've got chukar." Most of the time he will be right, since he is directing you to the bird's shelter, food and drink. These essential items will be evaluated separately, since I'll refer to them frequently in my attempt to use your understanding of the bird's behavior to advantage in hunting them.

Ideal chukar terrain contains a canyon, a small year-round stream or spring and several hundred feet of hillside that rises in a series of crude benches topped by ten to forty feet of rimrock. Plateaus include hundreds of yards of flat terrain occupied by

Prime chukar terrain. Abundant cheat grass and sage are present in the foreground and on the lower slopes. The hills have abundant contours and verticality. They can be climbed, and there is a large lake directly behind the photographer.

windblown rock and scanty sage. Hillsides are covered with rocks, loose rock fragments (scree, talus), sand, dirt, brush and grasses. Chukar live in such apparently inhospitable terrain because of the protective benefits it provides them. They pass the night on open hillsides where their excellent vision and a sentinel bird provide early warning of approaching predators. The precise spot where chukar spend the night is called the roost. You won't find any home improvements at the site of the roost, just an unusually large amount of chukar excrement. And you may not find too much of that, since the consistency with which they use a single specific site varies from covey to covey. A roost for one covey may be a patch of hillside the size of a football field; for another, it may be a card table. When inclement weather arrives, the roost is moved higher up the hill so that the birds can use rock formations to block the wind and to provide shelter against rain and snow.

The need to avoid moist weather partially explains the chukar's preference for a high and dry environment. In fact, they don't have many other landscape options. Since chukar are intolerant of moisture, they can't survive in coastal timber, deep forests or any land receiving more than 25 inches of precipitation annually. Most hunters think that the birds' requirement for unobstructed vision also plays a role in their selection of this terrain. There are occasions, however, when trees do assume importance in the chukar's life. One hunter with unusually extensive experience in hunting upland game has noted chukar roosting in junipers and in pine trees. Another hunter has seen chukar, when fleeing hunters, dive into the near side of junipers, run through the lowest branches and fly out the far side – successfully blocking a shot.

Thus, they are found in dry terrain which is treeless, and if rocky ground is adjacent to sandy soil, they are more likely to occupy the former. They are located high in this landscape because rocky irregular hillsides provide hiding places against predators and weather. Steep cliffs permit these relatively weak fliers to *drop* abruptly rather than climb slowly to gain altitude, as they attempt to evade raptors. An essential component of chukar terrain is, therefore, verticality, not just rimrock.For example, in Eastern Oregon, on the breaks of the Snake River north of Huntington, there is little rimrock. The terrain consists of steep, rolling hill interrupted by numerous draws. Chukar roost at the heads of these draws and the verticality appears to be adequate, because the are is home to abundant chukar populations each year.

Chukar spend most of their daylight hours at middle and lower altitudes feeding and seeking water during summer and early fall They are most active throughout the morning and in late afternoon Studies carried out by wildlife biologists 40 years ago indicated that chukar were prone to wander and routinely travel long distance during the year (4,5). However, observations in two recent studie which utilized radio-tagged wild chukar, calculated values for home ranges in Eastern Oregon and West-Central Idaho which conflic with earlier conclusions (A bird's home range is the area of land uses in carrying out its normal daily activities)(11,12). Surprisingly the values derived, 43-63 acres, were similar in both regions an much smaller than suggested by earlier observers. The day to da range of the birds, 282 meters, was essentially the same in bot recent studies and was also smaller than expected (please note tha

A roost in a typical location: the site is exposed, rocky and drops away precipitously. The shotgun in the right foreground is pointing at it.

ese data provide no information regarding distances traveled to
id from roosts). The earlier studies utilized pen-reared birds
·leased into a new environment, so that a degree of dispersal may
ive influenced their results. The more recent work used wild birds
hich were trapped, tagged and released immediately back into
ieir home environment.

The more recent studies are certainly consistent with hunters'
oservations. All agree that the chukar is a very territorial bird. Find
covey, hunt it, but not too much, and the remaining birds with
ieir numerous offspring will be waiting for you in the same home
·ea next year.

As noted, chukar spend the night in the open on a steep hillside.
nder normal circumstances they do not seek deep cover at night,
id simply go to sleep in small groups at nightfall. If there happens
» be ample grass in the area, you may find a half dozen crude
owls, 4 to 6 inches in diameter, imprinted in the grass the next

*A closer look at the roost. The small curls of chukar stool seen in the
right upper quadrant of the picture are typically all that is seen at a
roost site. The dusting bowl and tracks seen in the left lower quadrant
are unusual.*

morning; however, the drying effect of wind and weather quickl
eradicate them. Chukar possess excellent vision, are clearl
comfortable in the open and probably maintain some form c
sentinel system at night. Several important chukar predators suc
as the bobcat, coyote and the great horned owl hunt efficiently a
night, so it is logical to expect chukar to maintain vigilance durin
these hours. Support for this speculation was provided by Stua
Love, wildlife biologist and advisor to Hanspeter Walter (13). H
remarked, in the course of our interview, that in order to avoi
disturbing nearby coveys, Walter briefly attempted to service h
chukar traps at night. Despite his precautions in approaching th
traps, he continued to flush coveys roosting in the vicinity. O
several occasions, Walter clearly observed a single bird flush fro
a rock perch – followed by an entire covey from a separate si
nearby.

Although they inhabit arid terrain and don't consume larg
quantities of water, chukar seek a year-round water supply an

*The breaks above the Snake River consistently harbor good populatio
of chukar due to abundant water and grasses in a climate that favo.
these birds.*

lerefore, always roost in some proximity to water. During nesting eason in California, all chukar were detected within one mile of a ermanent water source (6). 72-93 percent of birds were within ne-half mile of water. During the hottest season (July - eptember), the birds spent much of the day around water and 92 ercent of the 189 broods observed, were detected within a quarter f a mile of water.

California and other states have had to supplement scanty local vater supplies with guzzlers in order to establish and maintain cceptable bird populations. These are artificial watering devices; irge tanks placed in the ground which provide water during dry eriods for small animals and birds. They are usually surrounded by 'ire to exclude larger animals, such as sheep and cattle, and they re strategically located to facilitate their use by chukar. It was oted in California that guzzlers sited on the flat or at the bottom of anyons received less use than those located just below the crest of

nother view of the terrain adjacent to the Snake River in northeastern regon. Little rimrock is encountered here; however, these apparently ently rolling hills are actually astonishingly steep and provide numerable opportunities for swift vertical chukar takeoffs.

a range or on small benches overlooking canyons (6). That is, th
chukar preferred water sources which were elevated and o
irregular ground, the environment in which they are mo.
comfortable.

Chukar arrive at watering sites from shortly after sunrise t
mid-morning. Adult birds and large juveniles arrive earlier an
spend more time around water than do hens with broods. All bire
seek shelter of some kind nearby: brush if available, or shac
provided by rocky outcroppings. It wasn't possible to assess th
frequency with which individual birds drank in Californi.
however, observations in Washington indicated that one drink a da
sufficed for nesting hens in spring. In summer and fall they dran
once or twice daily and required but a few minutes to meet the
needs (5).

*A small spring has been tapped with a plastic pipe. It feeds into a sturd
metal container which has been fenced to exclude horses and cattle. Thi
is the equivalent of a guzzler in parts of the arid West.*

3

THE CHUKAR DIET

Chukar eat practically everything. The vegetation in chukar prevalent areas features a mixture of brushes, grasses and non-grass herbs (forbs). Sagebrush is the most prevalent of the brushes, but bitter brush, rabbit brush and horse brush are also found. Annual and perennial grasses form the bulk of the chukar's diet; however, the bird is not highly selective and consumes an extraordinary variety of grasses and forbs. Most authorities stress the importance of insects in the diets of young birds, but chukar don't entirely lose their appetite for insects as they mature. I inspect the crops of the birds I shoot in the hope that I may find clues regarding favored feeding sites in the area I'm hunting. I encounter small numbers of grasshoppers, ants, beetles and other unidentifiable insect parts in most of them.

Crop examination is not an idle pursuit. While hunting chukar in an extremely remote and arid part of eastern Oregon, one hunter unexpectedly encountered birds in an area he had thought lacked water, and, consequently, was not expected to hold birds. He shot two of the birds and, in their crops he discovered the oval bodies of what were unmistakably water bugs. He surmised that water bugs meant not only water, but calm or standing water, so he and his partner were encouraged to hunt and to explore the area further. They hunted with good success, and it wasn't until the fifth day that they came across the pool of water in a deep ravine that supported both water-bugs and chukar.

Cheat grass, *Bromus Tectorum*, is present throughout the Great

Basin and is the staple of the chukar's diet in this region. If you hunt in Nevada or southeastern Oregon you will target it when you seek feeding chukar. On the other hand, when you travel to the hill and rocky slopes above the Columbia River in Washington, or the John Day River in Oregon, you will want to explore the margins of alfalfa and grain fields, since chukar may partake of these crops when they are available. Chukar are not particularly selective feeders even when dining on a single food. For example, Galbreath and Moreland found that when chukar fed on dandelions, they consumed the entire plant: leaves, seeds and flowering heads (5).

In southeastern California, 91 different food items were found in the crops of 87 chukar sampled. The seeds of Russian Thistle were found to be a staple of the bird's diet in this area (6). Russian Thistle is an annual plant, introduced to North America from abroad, which thrives in areas where the native cover has been disturbed. Miscellaneous grasses were next in importance in the chukar diet. They were found during all seasons of the year and like the dandelion, the entire plant was consumed. During late winter and spring, grass leaves and stems were eaten, while during late summer-fall the seeds, residual bulbs and roots were consumed. Harper, et al (6), observed that perennial grasses were preferable to annuals in maintaining chukar populations because these birds adept at digging for their food with beaks and claws, were able to utilize the roots of perennial grasses from a previous growing season when faced with a failure of new growth caused by drought or other unfavorable climatic conditions.

In Washington, Nevada, and Oregon cheat grass leaves and seeds are the principal components of the chukar diet (4-7). Other grasses, dandelions, wheat, and miscellaneous fruits and seeds are found according to the season and local prevalence. Insects were detected in all seasons, but never constituted more than 10 percent by weight, of chukar crop contents in Washington, where grasshoppers were the most commonly encountered animal food. Other items found were ants, beetles, crickets and rodent feces. The latter were presumably mistaken for seeds.

Traces of sage leaves and seeds were found in the crops of percent of chukar examined during the fall in California. Sage eaves were consumed in trace amounts by 3.8 percent of chukar xamined in Nevada. In Washington, sage galls were found in the rop of a single bird killed in winter (4-6). In Oregon, traces of sage eaves were found in the crops of 5.7 percent of 140 birds xamined, and sagebrush galls were detected in 26 percent. Considering the abundance of this plant in the chukar's world, it is lear that sage is not an important food for chukar.

Cheat grass, in all of its stages of growth, is of such importance o the hunter that a brief review of its history and biological ehavior is in order. It is not indigenous to North America, but was ntroduced late in the 19th century. The precise mode of ntroduction is unknown; however, seeds were probably carried in he clothing of immigrants or on the hides of imported animals.

It is an annual grass which, after sufficient rainfall, appears as mall, slender shoots resembling ordinary lawn grass. This seedling tate persists until spring, when it grows to a height of 8 to 14 nches, flowers and sets fruit. It drops seeds, dries out and assumes s characteristic golden-yellow hue in June. The seeds sink into the oil and remain dormant until the fall rains provide moisture for ermination, and the annual cycle is completed. The emergence of he green shoots following rain in the fall has been termed greenup" and its occurrence has major implications for the chukar unter. At this time the dead yellow stalks of the parent plant and he young green shoots are both visible, with the former serving as readily detected marker for the most concentrated areas of young rass.

Cheat grass is extremely hardy and has taken root throughout nuch of the American West, particularly in the Great Basin area. It as successfully displaced native grasses and forbs weakened by vergrazing and by adverse climatic conditions. Cheat grass dries nd distributes its seeds into the soil earlier than native grasses and erennials. During summer and fall while residual stalks serve as uel for fires, the seeds remain safely in the protective cover of the arth. When range fires occur in cheat grass bearing lands, ubsequent years, therefore, see a profound increase in the relative ensity of this grass in burned areas. Thus, cheat grass is not only ardy, but provides both tinder for the destruction of its competitors and early seeds for its own survival (14).

4

CHUKAR REPRODUCTION

Chukar remain in coveys through the winter. Individual birds ave the covey to form monogamous pairs in early spring; they isperse in order to establish a territorial base for nesting. Pair rmation depends on the availability of sunlight, food and cceptably warm temperatures. In California, egg laying usually egins in March or April with hatching in May. In Oregon, Nevada nd Washington egg laying commences in April with hatching in ine. These dates are approximations since egg predation or dverse weather may disturb egg laying and hatching may occur as te as August (4-6). The chukar is a persistent nester and will nest aggressively after destruction of its nest or eggs. All ten of e birds monitored by Lindbloom, which lost their eggs to redators, renested successfully within an average time of 13 days 1). Chukar do not have a second brood after a successful hatch.

Nests are well concealed and located on hillsides in brush or nder rocks. They are described by Walter as "scraped depressions ned with feathers and the leaves and stems of nearby plants" veraging 7.4 cm. in depth and 18.9 cm. in width (12). Lindbloom oted that 43 percent of first nests were located under rocks and 57 ercent were found in grasses and shrubs, a distribution similar to at observed by Walter (11). He found that 87 percent of nests ced in a southerly direction, 78 percent of renests were placed nder rocks and that nesting success was greatest in rocky cover.

The incubation period is 24 days, and brood sizes are relatively rge, averaging 9-12 chicks in Nevada,13-14 in Washington and regon and 9 in California. These large brood sizes help to

compensate for an annual natural (non hunter related) mortality ra
for chukar estimated to be in excess of 50 percent (10). Chicks a
precocious. They leave the nest shortly after drying and are fleet
foot and adept at hiding within hours of birth. They can fly sho
distances within two weeks.

During the first two to four weeks of life, broods (chicks wi
one or both parents) are found in shrub and grass cover, not
rocks. They use bunch grasses and shrubs for protective cover, ar
consume a diet rich in insects. As chicks grow, the brood migrat
to higher altitudes and increasingly rocky cover. It is speculated th
this sequence occurs primarily because the young chicks, lackir
fully developed flight capability, can only hide to evade predator
Thus, movement to more exposed, rocky ground is delayed unt
they are capable of using flight as a primary method for avoidir
predators (5,11,12).

Heavy rainfall and cold weather during the hatch results
higher levels of chick mortality; however, it has not been possib

*Precipitation in chukar country is often very focal. It may be beneficic
or harmful to chick survival depending on when it occurs in relation t
the hatch.*

predict nesting success based solely on measures of seasonal
infall (4). Heavy rains may actually be more beneficial than
armful if they occur in early spring and contribute to excellent
ood conditions later. For example, total rainfall in Walter's study
ea was normal in 1997, 158 percent of normal for all of 1998 and
00% of normal in May 1998, a peak nesting month. Despite this,
hick survival in 1998 was as good or better than in 1997 (12).
ther regional weather factors, such as thunderstorms, temperature
xtremes and wind also affect chick survival. Serious losses are
tributable to egg and nest destruction by predators. Ravens,
nagpies, foxes and coyotes are the most frequently cited predators
n this regard. Little predation of chicks and older juveniles has
een observed.

Chukar predators include the coyote, great horned owl, prairie
alcon, golden eagle and Cooper's hawk; however, hunters and
ildlife professionals report few kills actually witnessed. The
egree to which predation contributes to adult chukar mortality is
ssentially unknown. The chukar is a very alert bird with excellent
ision, coloring which provides excellent camouflage and an
ffective sentinel system. Accordingly, when they are healthy,
redators have little success taking them. Game biologists report
hat sentinel birds give an alarm cry promptly when a raptor
opears. Each member of the covey immediately crouches in
lace, remaining motionless while the raptor is in view and for
everal minutes after its departure. Hunters report frequent sightings
f golden eagles and hawks stooping on chukar, but success is
arely observed.

Since chukar do not generally inhabit agricultural land, farm
ills by machinery have not been a problem. The chukar's aversion
o flight leads it to scurry across public roads in order to reach
ater, and I have seen large numbers of birds swarming across
ublic roads, especially at dusk, climbing back uphill from water
ources. Fortunately, these roads are not heavily traveled and road
ills are uncommon, except during heavy snows when birds may
emain at the roadside seeking grain spilled from passing trucks (5).

Bad weather may cause widespread damage to chukar of any
ge and is the most important determinant of each year's chukar

population. Combinations of excessive heat and drought, moisture/snow and cold have depleted large areas of Washington Nevada and Oregon of chukar at intervals in the past (4,5 Fortunately, this mobile and hardy bird will migrate into devastate areas from adjacent territories to restock the region.This is just on of those aspects of chukar behavior which have endeared the bir to game biologists in the West.

Additional favorable qualities include the bird's choice habitat: relatively infertile terrain where it doesn't compete wit valuable native species. It consumes an alien grass of r commercial value, inflicts no significant damage on agricultur crops, and it is a worthy adversary for the hunter. It is in no dang of being depleted by hunters, and, although population cycles occi naturally, it does a satisfactory job of replenishing itself; therefor it doesn't consume precious financial and manpower resources i restocking efforts.

Golden eagles are known to be chukar predators. This golden eagle wa encountered cruising the rimrock in prime chukar terrain.

5

IN THE FIELD

Equipped with a better understanding of the chukar's needs
regarding food, water and shelter, we returned the following season
to the Warner Valley to learn more about their behavior in the field.
As usual, mornings were devoted to waterfowl, but in the afternoon
we sought chukar. The east side of this valley is composed of a
massive rock wall, many hundreds of feet high, which rises rather
abruptly from a valley floor dotted with a few large lakes and
innumerable potholes. It was a very poor water year, and we were
early in the season, driving slowly each morning along the rocky
road at the base of these steep cliffs to access our favorite duck
hunting areas. Returning to camp the first morning, we were
surprised to encounter two coveys of chukar. We left the car to
inspect the area and found a dense fringe of bright green aquatic
plants, mixed with what appeared to be clover, along the margins
of the lake. We assumed that the birds had been feeding on this
fresh growth, which stood in bright contrast to the brown, sun
baked grasses surrounding it.

One afternoon while driving, we encountered a sentinel chukar
for the first time. It was perched on a large rock, several yards off
the road, between the road and the receding lake shore. We stopped
short of it, and since I was both driver and dog releaser, I was just
getting to my gun when the large covey it was monitoring flushed
from cover. The birds flew across the rutted dirt road in front of the
car toward the hillside and my hunting partner who, to his eternal
shame, didn't draw a feather. I had no chance at the main covey and
was startled to see two mature birds break cover and run directly

away from me toward the water a hundred yards away. I ran aft
them. The dry lake bed provided solid footing, and there were r
boulders, brush or scree to slow my progress. Since I am both o
and slow of foot, I was exhilarated to find myself gaining on bo
birds. Admittedly, they handicapped themselves by weaving bac
and forth as they ran; nonetheless, I was clearly gaining on the
after forty yards, when they flew. It took me a little while to sto
and to get off my shot, but I made a clean kill of the second bird

Subsequently, when I have recognized birds on the ground
have run after them if the terrain permitted it, or if my adrenal
surge was strong enough to overcome good judgment. Almost a
of the hunters interviewed for this book had attempted running
catch up with escaping chukar at one time or another. All agree
that it could be done, but not often, because the chukar isr
normally encountered on unobstructed ground. Also, since I hu
with a flushing dog which doesn't always heed my commands, I a
sometimes forced to run to stay near the dog or pass up a shot.

There is no doubt that alarmed chukar prefer to run or hi
rather than fly. This is very understandable given their genet
imprinting and parental training. Christianson studied young chuk
within hours of birth and drying of their feathers (4). When t
brood was deliberately scattered, he observed that the chicks fro
in place for 10 to 15 minutes, until calling reunited them with the
mother. As adults, an entire flock may freeze in place when alert
to the presence of a predator by the sentinel bird or confronted I
an immediate threat. Their markings, melding with the usu
background of rocky soil and brush, make immobility an effecti
means of avoiding detection. One may also speculate that chuk
avoid flight because they feel vulnerable in the air. The surface ar
of their wings is relatively small compared to their body mass. Th
are not strong fliers; the act of flying must be energetica
expensive for them. This reluctance to fly is overcome when th
are in steep terrain where they can utilize gravity to accelera
rapidly.

The intensity of their desire to hide from danger cannot
overemphasized. Several years ago, I explored the Owyhee Riv
area in southeastern Oregon for chukar and quail. I spent the fi

orning attempting, without success, to obtain permission to hunt
n one of the attractive ranches in the valley. In order to get some
xercise for myself and for my elderly Labrador retriever, I
andered along a stream on public land running through sand and
ge. I walked a mile and shot two mallards coming off the stream.
s I retraced my steps toward the car, I became aware that
mething was watching me. Glancing to my left, I saw a chukar's
ead abruptly disappear below a sandy berm. What? A chukar in
e middle of nowhere, on the flat and within minutes of shotgun
lasts in the area? Yes. My dog had failed to pick up their scent, I
ad ambled past them and they had held tight while observing me.
/hen I topped the berm, 30 chukar burst into the air and for the
rst time in my life I dropped a legitimate triple.

A few years ago we camped and fished along the Deschutes
iver in central Oregon. Early one morning we were treated to the
ght of chukar coming to water on the opposite side of the river.
ifty chukar appeared on top of an absolutely vertical rock face one
undred feet high. They paid no attention to us and ignored an open
rassy slope nearby which would have afforded them easy walking
ccess to the river. They also could have set their wings, sailed off
e cliff and made a comfortable landing on a sand spit below them.
istead, two by two, they proceeded to climb down the face of that
ck cliff, laboriously using claws and beaks to secure a grip on the
anty vegetation in crevasses along the way. If one lost its footing
d fell into the air, it still did not fly down to the water. It fluttered
s wings like a helicopter and returned to the rock face, where it
gained its purchase and continued its trek. Truly, this bird dislikes
ight.

When flushed, chukar rise rapidly with noisy wing beats often
ccompanied by a brief shrill high pitched cry. They don't gain
uch altitude, perhaps 5 to 15 feet. Then they level off and head
wnhill as soon as the terrain and hunters' positions permit.
hukar fly slowly and are relatively easy to shoot when rising from
e ground; however, when their flight path changes and they start
wnhill, the speed they attain constitutes a challenge for the most
xperienced hunter. Dropping off a hillside, they usually don't rise
all, but slip directly downhill and away, creating very difficult

shooting angles for the hunter balanced precariously on the hillside

Chukar avoid flying uphill and, of course, they are rarel required to do so. If approached from below, they simply run uphi out of range. This tendency is so pronounced that one experience hunter of my acquaintance has flatly stated that they are unable t fly uphill. This is not true, and I have seen them fly directly up an over a long hillside. But it is unusual; perhaps it occurs as a resu of disorientation caused by shots directed at flushing birds fror hunters below them.

After flushing, chukar fly downhill with set wings alternatin with brief bursts of rapid wing beating. Although they ma sometimes fly in a straight line for long distances, more often, soon as they clear a hilltop or rimrock and are out of range, the follow a long curving arc along the face of the slope. They select rocky open area and land with a brief flutter of wings. They ru uphill seeking cover and hide until they call, or move toward othe of the covey who are calling. When they reunite, they migra uphill seeking altitude, cover and safety.

6

LOCATING BIRDS

In my experience, this has been the toughest aspect of chukar unting. In many respects the bird's behavior is quite predictable: hukar are territorial and found in the same general areas from one ear to the next. They flee from threats by running uphill, flying ownhill or hiding. They are found near water early in the season nd in protected southeast facing slopes when cold weather arrives.

Within this framework of predictability there exists a degree of ariable behavior to which we apply the term biodiversity. For xample, some birds are given to frequent rally calling while others all very little or not at all. Some birds are out of the roost early, nd when killed, are found to have already filled their crops with resh greens while others, harvested later in the morning, haven't egun to feed. Whole coveys will display varied responses to being unted, even in the absence of hunting pressure. For example, one unter interviewed for this book has had exclusive access for many ears to a large private tract of land containing a healthy population f wild chukar. Although he is the only person hunting this roperty, this experienced and thoughtful fellow notes that the oveys he encounters display a remarkably varied response to him nd to his dogs. Some permit the close approach that one expects ith undisturbed birds, whereas others flush out of range with little pparent provocation.

Perhaps it is some as yet undetected aspect of this chukar iodiversity that accounts for their absences in terrain that appears be ideal chukar habitat. If you pay close attention and work at it, ou will soon find that your ability to recognize unproductive

habitat develops rapidly. Regrettably, the opposite is not true
Tracts of land that appear to be ideal will prove barren of bird
while a mile down the road land that appears identical, will harbo
good numbers of chukar. This is where you put in your time an
effort. Hiking potentially productive terrain and searching fc
chukar or chukar sign cannot be avoided. The suggestions whic
follow are designed to ease this burden.

A few years ago, a friend and I drove eight hours from home t
hunt an area recommended by an acquaintance who was a
experienced chukar hunter. As is usually the case, his directior
were rather imprecise, but I knew that he had encountered birc
south of the small ranching community which became our bas
The weather was mild and the terrain and water conditions wei
perfect; nonetheless, we encountered no birds after many hours c
driving and hiking. Strangely, we also saw no other hunters. W

*A mountain in southeastern Oregon which is home to an excelle
population of chukar. It faces east, exhibits good contours, contar
adequate vegetation and rocky outcroppings. Its best quality is a go
supply of water which can be recognized by the abundance of gre
foliage seen in most of its ravines.*

ncountered a road grader at work late in the day and stopped to
hat with him. He wasn't surprised to hear of our poor results since
é told us that an unusually prolonged spell of freezing weather had
illed virtually every chukar in the area two years earlier. We
1oved fifty miles the next day and found decent hunting, so that
ur ignorance cost us only one lost day, but I no longer leave home
ithout some information about conditions in the area I plan to
unt. I acquire this information by monitoring regional sporting
ublications and by phone calls to friends, local sporting goods
tores and BLM or Fish and Wildlife offices

Once you have established the fact that chukar are present, or
t least haven't been ravaged by any recent major natural disasters
ou can push on to establish camp in your intended hunting locale.
ince I want to develop a logical approach to hunting chukar in this
ook, let's assume, for illustrative purposes, that you are a relative
ewcomer to the sport. And, being new to this area, you are at a
isadvantage compared to those hunters who have hunted here on

4 *similar mountain in nearby northern Nevada. It exhibits excellent
erticality, rocky outcroppings and contour. Regrettably, there is no
vater and this means no vegetation and no chukar.*

a regular basis, or who have homes nearby. These hunters will have hunted and explored the area for years. They have learned where these territorial birds roost, and some of them even know when they are likely to be in specific locations at certain times of the day. I am acquainted with hunters who hunt geese or ducks in the morning, then, using trucks or ATVs later in the afternoon, they drive to areas of interest to hunt specific terrain briefly, and then rapidly move on to the next spot. Learning one area well can be very productive.

You don't possess this kind of information yet, so you have to do some driving to scout the terrain and to select a starting point for your first day of hunting. As you drive, it may occur to you that would have been smart to scout the area for birds before the season opened, since, in the distance, you can hear shots echoing off hillsides.

For several reasons, you probably made the right choice. You live, like most of us, in a large town many hours drive from good

A skiff of early snow highlights this ideal setting. The fall colors of the trees and the vegetation in the saddle seen in the center of the photograph betray the existence of plentiful groundwater.

hukar country. You have only two or three weeks vacation each ear, and your wife is astonishingly disinterested in hunting chukar. hen there is the issue of scouting efficiency. Covering the hukar's terrain is not exactly a walk in the park, and even game iologists haven't figured out how to do it efficiently. To quantify hukar populations they still depend on crude estimates obtained by riving the same routes each year, tallying the number of birds en, then comparing that count with counts performed in prior ears.

A simple but efficient first step in scouting by car involves a arch for tracks. Since you are driving in remote terrain, most of our time will be spent on dirt and gravel roads. When you pass rough areas that look likely to hold chukar, stop the car where ou find well defined ravines coming down to the road. Get out and ok for tracks in the dirt at the side of the road where the ravine rminates. You will find no tracks, or a few blurred tracks, at many

ere is good grass and sage around this large lake extending up to the lside where vertical rock walls are encountered. You can hunt this ea, but the cliffs cannot be climbed by humans and chukar readily cape by running uphill.

of these locations. Keep moving until you strike gold: numerou
fresh, well defined chukar tracks not masked by cattle's hooves. A
you look further, you will find that the tracks show up also acros
the road, but don't extend very far along the sides parallel to th
road. Congratulations, you have found chukar and a primar
traveling route.

You can't know whether the birds are above or below you, b
it is early in the day and you do know that the roost is above yo
so you opt for a climb. The ravine will split and peter out as yc
climb; they all do, so reassess the terrain as you go. Using contou
and brush to conceal your progress, keep looking for tracks ar
pick the brushiest ravines at each leg of your journey. The soil ge
rockier as you gain altitude and tracks are harder to detect, so pa
close attention to any bare spots you encounter, no matter ho
small. As you progress, look for birds feeding on a flat or a bow
and you may run right into them, traveling in the opposite directio
I have had this experience several times. It is very challengin
because the birds will have sensed your presence and hidden. Whe
you walk into the middle of them, they explode on all sides in
relatively confined space, and it takes a cool head to sho
accurately.

It isn't always clear to me why chukar select some of the rout
that they seem to prefer. Some of their highways are quite unusua
Several years ago, a friend and I hunted an area in Southeaste
Oregon and enjoyed some success in the morning. We paused
midday on sandy, flat land between rocky hills and a large, shallo
lake three miles away. As we ate our sandwiches, we wander
around the car, watered the dogs and ambled over to the edge of
remarkably deep and narrow, dry gully. It was more than 35 fe
deep, and as we stood there discussing the inferior quality of o
fare, a veritable horde of chukar came marching into view acro
the smooth, sandy bottom directly below us. We couldn't belie
our eyes, knew it was a mirage, but that didn't prevent us fro
rescuing the guns from the rig.

What now? There was no way to approach them witho
alarming them, so we decided to alarm them without approachin
them. We dropped a rock in their midst. Instantly, there wasn't

*his is ideal chukar terrain located far from any town and on a private
inch. Despite intensive efforts, we found neither chukar nor signs of
hukar here, although we have taken birds within a few miles of this
)ot. The absence of birds in such apparently ideal locations will
ustrate every chukar hunter from time to time.*

ngle bird visible and none flew. We waited 20 minutes and never
iw a bird move. Finally, I made my way very carefully down the
de of the canyon, holding onto roots and rocks with my lab in
w. Reaching bottom, I started to feel silly, thinking that they had
:obably run off somewhere, since none flushed during my descent.
moved a few yards along the bottom, then started to climb up
ward a patch of brush when they flushed simultaneously from
ultiple locations on all sides of me. Since I was clinging to a rock
all at the time I managed only one shot which, mercifully, was
:curate, but my companion never raised his gun because the birds
ayed low in the gully until they were out of range. The lesson here
that when you encounter chukar in unexpected locations it may
)t be that they favor the area; they may simply be en route to a
:tter place. In this instance, further exploration revealed that they
ere traveling back from a visit to a cattle watering trough half a
ile away.

At certain times of the day, notably in late afternoon, chuka may be encountered along roadsides. They seem attracted to thes sites in order to gather grit for their gizzards. This organ is remarkably muscular component of the stomach which grinds seec and other materials into a pulp which is then absorbed in the sma intestine. The gizzard performs the same function as the teeth c animals, and grit is thought to aid this process. The next time yo clean a chukar, cut through the center of the gizzard. You can miss it. It is the size, shape and firmness of a chestnut. Within th stomach cavity, the tube-like structure running through the cente of this muscular organ, you will find grit mixed with vegetatioi The grit is composed of a homogeneous population of hard stone from 2 to 4 mm in diameter, and there is a surprising amount of i

Since chukar inhabit rocky terrain which surely contains sma hard stones, it is rather surprising that they take the risk of seekin grit at roadsides. One may speculate that 2-4mm very hard stor

A chukar's stomach opened lengthwise to display the gravel-filled upp stomach and the heavily muscled lower stomach, called the gizzar Samples of the gravel are displayed on both sides of the stomach. Th stones nearest the dime are the size most commonly encountered.

fragments may simply be less abundant in certain terrain. Their absence may induce chukar to grit at roadsides, where such particles are present in greater abundance and, therefore, obtained with much less effort. This is consistent with the observation that gritting doesn't occur every day, and isn't observed at all in some areas. This is a rather long-winded explanation for why road scouting late in the day will be productive in some areas and not in others.

Since you are already in your vehicle and driving comfortably, with the companionship of your dog and a good friend, it will occur to you that road hunting might be a productive undertaking. Generally, it is not as effective as hiking across appropriate terrain, but if you are new to an area and want to learn the basic terrain, a survey by car is a reasonable starting point. However, you aren't going to see much country if you drive at the very slow speeds required for flushing birds. Driving at normal speeds will flush few

This location contains rimrock, extensive cheatgrass and some water, but don't hunt it. The monotonously even terrain provides no cover for your approach. Chukar will see and hear you, and you will never see them.

chukar. This is probably because normal speeds catch birds by surprise and they react by freezing in place. Very slow speeds, 5 mph or less, on back country roads give the birds more time to detect your presence, become nervous and to run or fly away. Some hunters report success in locating birds by car, then releasing their dogs and hunting on foot. But most of these hunters are not new to the areas they patrol, and they have a pretty good idea of where they will encounter birds before they leave the barn. Finally, unless you are physically handicapped or tired by your activities earlier in the day, road hunting can be pretty boring. So your goal this first day is to focus on identifying the locations containing rimrock and water. When you have done this, select a site where the two are reasonably close, then get out of the truck and hunt it.

While you are hunting, you are also scouting. There is no avoiding the fact that, to achieve success in chukar hunting, you will be putting in lots of time and effort on foot. You must know

Contrast this terrain with that in the previous photograph. Hills are similar in steepness of slope, profusion of grasses and availability of water; however, the ravines and rocky outcroppings here provide an irregular contour which provides the conditions for a concealed approach to the birds.

ow the land really lies, and this can't be determined from the road.

Early in the season, at some time in the morning, chukar either fly or walk to water. They don't really fly, they just drop off a steep pitch, set their wings and glide down silently. They will remain close to water for extended periods of time; particularly when it is very hot and dry. The most nutritious greens are found at the waters edge, and in extremely dry years, such growth may be their only source of fresh green leaves and shoots. Chukar will remain in such an area for most of the day provided that there are rock formations, brush, or sage to provide cover for protection against intruders.

In this regard, water sources such as small springs and creeks on hillsides are preferred locations for the birds because they are so closely associated with rocks, and their riparian areas are less likely to have been damaged by livestock since they are relatively inaccessible. Water holes created by man-made dams in dry areas are much less attractive because they are usually located on flat, bare terrain away from rocky areas, and livestock have browsed

All of the basic ingredients to sustain chukar are found here, but there are too many junipers. Chukar generally avoid trees, and if you do encounter birds here they will use the trees to evade you and your shots.

and trampled nearby brush. Furthermore, by the opening of chukar season in early fall, most of these water holes are much reduced due to consumptive and evaporative water loss. This leaves behind a rim of barren mud and clay. No self-respecting chukar risks exposing himself to predators in such an open area.

Next, take the following approach. Park at a distance from the water source, so that you are out of sight and hearing of these alert birds. Do not slam the door, and do not lock it with the remote control on your key chain. If the water is a pond, climb high enough to approach it from above or from the side. Walk as quietly as possible using brush, berms, and rock walls to conceal your approach. When you reach the water, look for tracks then carefully explore the cover in the area for a hundred yards or so. Look further if likely cover exists. If no birds are found, turn uphill. When chukar abandon water, they will generally graze uphill in the direction of their roost. They may not travel far, and may return to water later in the day.

These hills have a rich crop of grasses, but their verticality is mediocre, they are relatively far from water, and their rock formations are at the bottom of the hills. Few chukar are found here.

Pursue a diagonal course up the hill, and position yourself pproximately two shotgun ranges from your partner. If you both ave dogs be sure to separate far enough so that the dogs' ranges lon't overlap. Where possible, use draws and small ravines along he way. They provide cover for you and contain more nourishing orage than open slopes at this early season. As you hunt toward the imrock and leave the water behind, recall that chukar, feeding at distance from moisture, focus on seeds, roots and insects. Explore atches of dried cheat grass stems where birds may be scratching or seeds and always look for fresh droppings. Since chukar require over seek out potential sources of food which are intermixed with ome brush, sage and rocks. When you are away from water you re always seeking chukar forage, because that is where the birds vill be found. Although chukar have an absolute requirement for vater, they can be satisfied with small amounts acquired in

his is a rocky mound on a hillside three miles south of the hills in the revious photograph. They appear similar, but they differ in two nportant respects: there is a small perennial seep nearby, and the regular rock formations on top provide adequate verticality and cover. here are always chukar here.

Sometimes you just get lucky and can count your blessings. We encountered chukar, quail and pheasant in this small jewel of a valley in eastern Oregon.

minutes. Satisfaction of their fuel requirements requires many hours. The substances they consume frequently contain a high percentage of material of negligible nutritional content. Their food is often scarce or widely scattered and the climbing, scratching and pecking required to obtain it consumes energy. As a result, chukar spend most of their day foraging. That's why it behooves you to be able to identify and locate such areas.

If you reach the rimrock without encountering birds, you and your partner should follow a course parallel to the rimrock, one on top and one below, for a predetermined distance or time. Now you are both hunting chukar and seeking the only reliable sign of a roost: large quantities of stool which may be encountered above or below the rimrock. Hunt back downhill, moving obliquely, and then compare notes with your partner. If you encountered birds, you are in business. If you found tracks near water, evidence of a roost or fresh droppings the birds are there; you just missed them. If you encountered none of these you're in unproductive territory. Move on.

If you found signs of chukar but saw no birds and want to hunt the same area again, analyze what you might change in your approach. Try a different area, start high and come down on the water, or try a totally different approach. Consider setting an ambush for the birds by the water. This can be particularly effective when applied to a focal water source, such as a spring, as opposed to a larger body of water like a lake or year-round stream. Conceal yourselves in nearby rocks or in a small blind composed of sage and brush, and be set up in time to welcome the first arrivals. Since chukar may water at any time between dawn and mid morning, you will have to be an early riser. I have been told by hunters who have tried it, that the birds frequently call quietly to each other as they approach water, emitting a slow and quiet *tuk, tuk,* sound. The obvious drawbacks to this approach include not only the early hour, but the fact that it may be hours before birds arrive...if they do.

Stop and talk with every hunter you encounter. Upland bird hunters are generally open and friendly. They are highly susceptible to favorable comments directed at their dogs, and any information or advice you receive may be useful. While you won't receive much information regarding the precise whereabouts of your quarry, most hunters will provide accurate information about areas to avoid, and this is very helpful information.

Continue to seek productive looking terrain. This morning you hunted a particularly nice combination of water and rimrock. Your discovery of a small, focal water source in proximity to rimrock early in the season permitted you to be focused on a small area, while hunting and scouting new territory. On the other hand, your travels this afternoon have brought you, late in the day, to very different terrain. Before you stretches a long, narrow valley surrounded by high hills topped with rimrock on each side. There is a long lake occupying the valley floor. Where should you start your hunt when confronted by endless tracts of apparently excellent chukar habitat bordered by a stream or lake providing unlimited access to water?

The answer to this question lies in the resources you possess. If you are in excellent physical shape and are an experienced hunter with well trained dogs, you drive to a likely looking spot, open the door and follow the dogs. Their noses will do the deciding for you. If your conditioning is a little short of superb, your dog sometimes loses the scent or fails to hold a point, and your experience isn't too extensive, there are a few steps you can take that will improve your chances. In this situation, put Fido in your canoe or small boat, crank up the electric motor and cruise along the shore looking and listening for birds in the morning. If your dog has a good nose he may even point birds, or get birdy, as you travel in maximum silence. Ignore birds as you glide by. Then, out of sight and hearing, put into shore and work fast to get above them.

It has been a long day. With about an hour of daylight remaining, drive to several locations with good looking terrain, get out of the car and start listening.

7

TACTICS

Biologists observing chukar in the wild and in prolonged aptivity have described the calls given by chukar. Fourteen calls ave been described for birds studied in captivity (15,16); however, ie hunter usually hears only two: a raucous, high-pitched squeal mitted by some birds when flushed and the rally call.

The rally call is the loudest, most commonly encountered call, nd is the one that has led to its species name. The word chukar is erived from the sound of the rally call, and the onomatopoetic elationship between name and call is maintained even when the vord chukar is traced back to its Hindustani (cakor) and Sanskrit cakora) roots. Stokes stated that, at low intensities, the call ounded like *chuck, chuck, chuck* with a pause between each call. .t higher intensity the call became *perchuck* with emphasis on the econd syllable, and at highest intensity and volume it sounded like *huckara* repeated three times without a pause (15).

It is a unique call, not easily confused with that of any other ird, and may carry for hundreds of yards. It is heard most onsistently at dawn, mid morning and dusk and, therefore, may be elpful in marking the birds in proximity to their roost. The call is eard at random during the day in the spring when it is given by 1ales either defining their territory or in conflict with other cocks. t is heard with predictable reliability when a covey has dispersed fter being flushed. After an initial period of quiet, chukar use this all to assist in reassembling the covey. It also may be used as an larm call. On more than one occasion, when I have been spotted

by birds after emerging abruptly from concealment, I hav
provoked a rally call followed by an immediate scramble uphill an
away.

As noted earlier, wildlife biologists have been frustrated in thei
attempts to locate chukar and to quantify population densities in th
wild. Forty years ago attempts were made, using captive bird
trucked around the countryside, to induce calling in wild birds as
means of locating them. The captive birds proved uncooperative, s
biologists recorded their calls and broadcast them from trucks
horseback and hand carried recorders (17). It was estimated tha
wild birds responded to only 50-60 percent of the calls playec
Adults with broods and nearby birds seemed not to respond at all

In 1960, Williams studied factors influencing the spontaneou
rally calling rates of 20 pairs of chukar released at one site in Utah
He confirmed that the greatest frequency of calling occurred i
early morning, from shortly before dawn up to mid-morning, an
again late in the afternoon, from 45 minutes before to 15 minute
after sunset. The frequency and duration of spontaneous rall
calling was found to be influenced by many factors: social contact
within and between coveys, the presence of raptors, hig
temperatures, wind and rain. Williams concluded that th
spontaneous rally calling of the wild chukar could not be use
reliably as an index of abundance for the bird (18,19), but tha
doesn't mean that listening at dawn and at dusk won't provide th
alert hunter with valuable information.

Most of the hunters interviewed for this book had tried callin
as a means of locating chukar. They all used the type of cal
activated by a rubber bellows, and results were mixed. No on
claimed great success, and the reasons given for failure were simila
to the observations of wildlife biologists. Chukar located nearb
never returned the call. When distant birds returned the call, i
proved very difficult to pinpoint their location due to the echoin
of sound off irregular hillsides. Furthermore, the *chukara* sound o
the rally call possesses a peculiarly hollow, haunting quality that i
quite unlike the harsh rasp of a mallard or the sharp whistle of
quail. This quality adds to the difficulty of precisely locating
distant call.

Half of the hunters found the call not helpful, and none considered it a highly effective tool. One wryly observed that he thought the primary effect of his calling was to alert the birds to his presence. Another hunter found that, over the years, birds in some areas consistently returned his calls while birds in other areas did not. This phenomenon held true during three decades of hunting the same terrain. It became apparent that those who found the call of least use were those who hunted most actively, and who had greatest confidence in their dogs' ability to find birds. These hunters had employed the calls while actively hunting in good habitat, hoping to locate birds in their immediate area, but nearby chukar did not respond.

Those hunters whose goals were more modest, and who used calling as a scouting tool, thought the call useful. They drove roads in unfamiliar country, usually in the early morning, marked the locations where their calls were answered, then drove on. If they thought the terrain was suitable, they returned later that day, or another day, to hunt the area. They didn't call when they returned in order to avoid alerting the birds. They didn't expect to find the birds in precisely the same location; however, they felt that the knowledge that birds were definitely in the area to be hunted was quite helpful.

Let's return to our hunter. You have listened for calling chukar for 10 minutes without success, so you turn to the calls which you purchased before leaving home. You have both the rubber bellows activated call made by Lohman (4500 Doniphan Drive, Neosho, MO. 64850) and the mouth operated call made by Faulk (616 18th St., Lake Charles, La.). Try the bellows call first because the sound produced is good, and less skill is required to operate it. Start with brief soft calls. Put a space between calls, then link them as volume rises and use a rising and falling cadence. Call for 4 to 8 seconds at a time then wait for 20-30 seconds for a reply.

If calling doesn't elicit a response, a loud noise or an unusual call may be productive. One hunter gets consistently better responses with his crow call than with his chukar call. Another prefers a coyote call (rabbit in distress), and others commented that any loud noise, even the slamming of a car door may startle birds

into a brief rally call. It is dusk, so you return to camp encourage
by the fact that you have found good looking terrain, and that som
of it contains chukar since your calling has elicited a few distar
responses. Tomorrow you will hunt it.

This leads to an important subject: changes observed in chuka
behavior as the season progresses. The chukar season is, in reality
three separate and reasonably distinct seasons: early (befor
greenup), greenup, and late (snow/cold/wind). The early seaso
extends from opening day to greenup when, following sufficier
rainfall, the green shoots of cheat grass and other grasses emerge
The early season is characterized by warm weather and the birds
absolute requirement for water. During the warmest days i
unmolested, they will drink in the mid morning and late afternoor
They will form flocks consisting of several coveys and spend mos
of the day browsing, resting and napping. They rest during th
hottest hours in shade and, when resting, they come together in
more condensed grouping and, when feeding, they disperse.

During the early season, they are focused on water, but not o
specific foods. They consume whatever is on or in the grounc
seeds, fruits, insects and roots. Therefore, while they may focus o
areas containing the dried stalks of cheat grass where they scratc
for seeds, they are just as likely to feed in any areas of fresh growt
such as that which may be found in ravines, dried watercourses an
on the fringes of standing water or streams.

For the hunter, the large flocks encountered early in the seaso
are exciting. The ability to factor in water sources, especially foca
springs or ponds, in planning the hunt is a major advantage. On th
negative side, the majority of birds in these large flocks will b
young, small birds; it requires experience and discipline to avoi
shooting them. Some hunters deliberately avoid the early season fo
fear that their dogs may be bitten by the Western Diamondbacl
rattlesnake, which is prevalent in chukar country. Higl
temperatures may create problems for both dogs and hunters. Dry
dusty weather may impair scenting conditions, and if you mus
carry sufficient water for your dogs, your own physical capabilitie
may be stressed. Finally, there are skilled chukar hunters who avoi

e early season because they feel that the preponderance of young, isceptible birds and the chukar's dependence on water makes the unting too easy to be challenging. These hunters have great respect or the chukar as an adversary and believe that efforts should be irected at harvesting only mature birds.

When greenup occurs, we enter the second chukar season. At is time, you want to concentrate less on water sources and more n locating the green grass shoots which chukar depend upon for oth food and water. Early showers and dew frequently occur in a atchy manner in chukar country, so new grasses may be abundant one area but absent in another nearby. Accordingly, you must ecide if greenup exists in the area you hunt. It isn't difficult. Just ok closely at the ground for shoots of green grass which look just ke the stuff growing in your lawn, albeit much more sparsely. If doubt, seek out patches of the dried stalks of cheat grass and rutinize the ground. The seeds in the soil sprout rapidly given lequate water and soil temperature. If rainfall of sufficient agnitude occurs late in the summer, greenup may even be iderway when the chukar hunting season opens. After greenup, ese grasses comprise the major part of the chukar fall and winter et (4,5).

Chukar require remarkably small volumes of water and this quirement can be met by the moisture contained in these fresh, een shoots. Since they no longer must travel to water, they may end the day traveling only as far from the roost as needed to otain adequate nutrition; although, if undisturbed, they will ntinue to travel to water until it freezes or hunters intrude. unting pressure, as well as poorly understood natural forces, lead a fragmentation of the large flocks found at the beginning of the ason, so that the number of birds in the groups encountered after eenup are smaller.

Articles written on this subject usually advise the hunter, at eenup, to look for the birds "on top." Well, I'm an obedient llow, and for some years routinely hiked to the top of whatever lls I was hunting and looked for birds there. Sometimes I found rds, but I couldn't help noticing that the grass and brush on the lltops, was usually less abundant than that found in patches below the top. After gaining more experience and discussing the subject with other hunters, I came to realize that the birds were not necessarily above rimrock after greenup, they simply were found at generally higher elevations due to the fact that they no longer had to travel down to a water source below their roost in order to take on water every day. They are now distributed according to the location of their roost, their food and the hunting pressure which pushes chukar to higher elevations.

To hunt successfully during this season, avoid the well-traveled trail (other hunters), seek roosts and look for birds feeding all day long. Look for chukar in high basins and bowls containing sage or brush mixed with grasses. That is, islands of terrain that provide cover, food and shelter from a wind that grows colder as the season progresses. Now the days are shorter and colder, and the chukar can no longer afford to loaf around in cover during the middle of the day.

The third and final season is ushered in by nasty weather. Obviously, this season will be more pronounced in northern Idaho, Washington and Oregon than in southern California. Cold, wet or snowy weather, especially when mixed with wind, forces the birds to change the location of their roosts. As noted, chukar usually roost in the open on hillsides, but when sufficiently adverse weather conditions arrive they start to form larger groupings again, and they seek the protection of rocky outcroppings and niches within rimrock which afford protection. In terrain lacking rimrock they move to the brush in steep heads of draws. They seek south facing slopes which are warmer and receive more sunlight. The extra sunlight also favors the growth of vegetation.

The effect of snow on hunting conditions depends on its duration, its character and the amount that accumulates. Hunting in a few inches of fresh snow can be very exciting. Scenting conditions are good, dogs can run all day, birds are more readily visible and following fresh tracks is great sport. The birds' routines are not much disturbed; they can easily scratch and feed through few inches of fresh snow.

Heavier snowfall requires more extensive adjustments for both hunter and bird. Chukar will roost at higher elevations among rock heavy brush for protection against moisture, wind and cold. In e morning following a heavy snowfall rocks, sage and other ushes will have accumulated snow and islands of bare ground are und at their downwind bases. Chukar tracks are found in a ndom pattern as the birds move directly from one bare patch to other: dusting, resting and consuming fresh grasses. Since water abundant and they are threatened by moisture and cold, they avel as little as possible. Only hunger forces them out of the roost.

Now this sounds like a pretty good arrangement for the hunter. you are at all familiar with the area you wish to hunt, you can adily figure out where the birds are going to be in these onditions. The problem lies in getting there. Since we are talking out four to eight inches of snow, we are well into the season. unting pressure has driven the birds far from good roads, and

heavy snowstorm creates a beautiful landscape scene, and it is said y some) to drive the birds down to lower elevations making them more cessible. That may be true under certain circumstances, but my perience has been that the snow covers everything, the birds go to ound, and the footing, which was difficult when dry, becomes wnright perilous when obscured by snow.

most dirt and gravel roads won't be passable for any distance, s
you are in for a long, unpleasant trip to reach these chukar.

It is unpleasant because the snow makes the footing slipper,
and for the most part, you can't tell what you are stepping on. Th
is not fun on steep, uneven ground. Finally, the sun usually mak
an appearance during the days after heavy snowfall. It melts tl
snow surface which then freezes during the night to provide a cru
the next morning. Breaking through this crust makes the hikir
even more difficult for hunters and rapidly leads to bleedin
abraded legs and paws for your dogs. I've tried it with no succe
or enjoyment and now remain in camp with a good book becau:
I know that better days are coming.

As temperatures rise and sunlight becomes more abundar
snow melts first on south facing slopes and chukar travel there
enjoy the sun and exposed grasses. I have read many articles
sporting publications which describe this event as providing a
excellent opportunity for hunters. They talk about a well defin
snow line with an accompanying sketch showing hunters workir
along a hillside just below snow which covers the hill with
homogenous coating of white all the way to the summit. Tl
inference is that the birds won't enter the snow; therefore, tl
hunters have them trapped in the open area below it. Don't ho
your breath waiting for this to happen.

What actually occurs is that bare ground is exposed in a patcl
fashion according to the depth of the snow, nature of the soil ar
degree of sun exposure. Higher elevations contain more rock ar
receive more wind, so that these patches tend to appear there fir:
Contrary to that ice cream cone of a hill, you end up walkir
through deeper snow down low to reach these patches, but its wor
it when you can, because the birds will be there: in the sun, out
the wind and dining.

For each day's hunt, it is helpful to review four primary chuk
hunting variables:
1. Which season is it: before greenup, after greenup or late?
2. Are you hunting the most appropriate terrain?
3. How heavily have the birds been pressured by other hunte

this area?

4. Should you modify your hunting tactics today as a result of rrent, or anticipated weather conditions?

Subjects one and two have been addressed in earlier chapters, t hunting pressure deserves a few comments. Hunting causes ukar to become spookier: they become more wary and alert, so it they run or flush with less provocation. Accordingly, they hold s well for you and for your dogs, and it is harder to get a decent ot. Earlier, I described a trip to southeastern Oregon during which experienced great frustration due to our inability to get close to birds. In retrospect, we recognized that those birds had been avily hunted, and our poor results could have been predicted if had been more experienced. The season had been open for three eks, there was a single, well marked road into the area and the st terrain was extensively crisscrossed with well maintained dirt ids serving the local mining interests. It was too accessible. This good example of why successful chukar hunters often start their nt with a climb into territory beyond the reach of the average nter.

Although the chukar is a highly territorial bird and can be ind in the same general area from year to year, most experienced nters agree that sufficient hunting pressure can drive birds from ir normal location. How much pressure? Hunters who hunt the ne area with a days rest between hunts, report that the birds are arly more wary on the second hunt and flush out of range on the rd. You can imagine the effect on your success if one or more oups of hunters have recently preceded you in the area you oose to hunt.

It is not always easy to assess the degree of hunting pressure. ou are in an area which has traditionally produced good chukar pulations and has been touted in the newspaper as prime country chukar this year, you know that you are going to have company. ou hunt such an area, despite knowing that the birds have been essured, you will need to be more circumspect in concealing urself and in your approach to the birds. Also consider climbing more remote areas, using heavier shotgun loads for longer range ots at nervous birds and tightening the choke.

An abundance of pickup trucks parked just off the road a[?] campers scattered among the junipers are also poor prognos[?] signs. Two years ago we hunted a moderately remote valley central Oregon. We were delighted to have the area to ourselv[?] and to encounter good hunting for a variety of birds. One year lat[?] we decided to start the season there, and we were stunned to fi[?] four motor homes scattered through the valley. We didn't bother hunt it..

It is normally good policy to avoid attractive country read[?] seen from heavily traveled roads, but there can be surprises. A f[?] years ago, my partner and I rested in the truck late one afternoc[?] while my younger son pursued quail he had seen cross the road. [?] first shot at the quail flushed a nearby covey of chukar, and off [?] went. We hunted that open hillside in plain view of the main ro[?] and had excellent success. There are exceptions to every chuk[?] rule.

To avoid pressured birds, many hunters seek remote, l[?] hunted areas, or simply hike high and far at the outset, leaving l[?] fit and ambitious hunters behind. This is the basis for t[?] commonest complaint I heard regarding vehicles such motorcycles and ATVs. Encountering hunters on these rigs afte[?] long, tiring hike to get away from others was described depressing and annoying. Hunters on foot felt that reaching ga[?] this way demeaned the hunt and the hunter. They felt that it was[?] sporting and that the chukar was a magnificent bird that deserv[?] to be hunted in a more sporting manner. "Chukar ought to earned" was a constant refrain, but the same hunters specifica[?] mentioned that they had no objection to the use of the conveyances by the handicapped or elderly.

Wind of mild or moderate degree favors the hunter. It carr[?] scent without breaking it up and provides the hunter with a route follow in approaching likely cover. High winds, on the other har[?] scatter scent and make the birds more skittish. Sustained high win[?] force the birds to seek shelter in the lee of rock formations, denser brush or at canyon bottoms. A hunting acquaintance of mi[?] has maintained a camp in the same valley for many years. Wh[?] winds of 25 miles per hour arise unexpectedly and roar through [?]

lley from the south, he is able to take advantage of it because he
ows exactly where the chukar will huddle for protection. Many
nters, however, don't enjoy hunting in strong winds because of
: poor scenting conditions and the greater tendency of the birds
flush out of range.

Later in the season, when a storm moves through, it is
quently violent and associated with wind and rain or snow. Such
rms usually don't last long and when they pass, chukar give the
-clear and come out to feed and chatter right on the heels of the
rm. Examine your next bird closely and you will understand the
sis of this urgency. They possess virtually no subcutaneous fat,
ch as may be found on ducks and geese, to insulate them from the
ld and to provide sustenance if unable to feed for several days.
ok carefully at the feathers. For birds living at high altitude in the
nd and cold, they are pretty scantily clad. While the chukar
otects itself from cold and wind by fluffing his feathers to
:rease their insulation value, huddling with his family out of the
:ments and facing south into whatever sunlight may exist; his
imary defense lies in obtaining nourishment. Since there often
1't abundant food in his environment, in all but the most adverse
nditions, he's out early and eating all day long.

The chukar is a shy, wary bird often accompanied by a vigilant
ntinel as it pursues its daily activities. Early in the year, when the
vey is composed primarily of juvenile birds, and their elders have
d eight or nine months to forget the sounds of dogs and shotguns,
:y may be approached once without much caution, but tread
ftly thereafter. They will see you and they will hear you. For most
us who hunt with a companion and one to two dogs, this means
nsidering ways to conceal our approach most of the time. It
:ans that a hunt across the top of an open table which was
ccessful early in the season will fail later due to lack of cover, and
obably should be avoided. It means careful analysis of terrain to
hunted, so that you are exposed as little as possible. The
owledgeable hunter automatically takes advantage of rocky
itcrops, ravines, tall vegetation and irregular land contours to
nceal the sight and sound of his approach.

It is hard to know just how color-conscious the birds may be;

however, there aren't many bright colors in their environment. S
unless you are hunting during big game season most hunters thi
that it is wise to leave the orange hat and vest in the rig. Noise
any kind is counterproductive. Hand signals can be arranged wi
your partner before starting to hunt, and when audit
communication becomes necessary consider using a crow or chuk
call to get your partner's attention. Dogs and whistles are a tou
issue, but bear in mind that it's much more important for you to
hidden than it is for your dog to be concealed.

Hunters using multiple dogs tell me that, although th
acknowledge the importance of a stealthy approach to game, this
difficult to accomplish when tracking several fast moving dogs
rough country. For them, concealment becomes critical when t
dogs go on point. Then they must analyze where the birds are like
to be holding relative to the dog on point and relative to t
surrounding terrain. They can usually predict the direction in whi
the birds will want to fly when flushed, and they approach
quietly and quickly as possible to intercept this route. Naturally,
the season progresses, they must be even more circumspect in the
approach.

Most hunters climb to gain altitude at the outset of a hunt,
part to avoid other hunters, but also in order to be able to hunt dov
on chukar. Approaching birds from above frustrates their preferr
means of escape: running uphill. Pressured from above, the bir
can fly down or run laterally, but all agree that they hold long
when a menace approaches from above. It is not clear why this
true. Perhaps their first instinct is to move toward their roost, whi
is usually above them. When they find their route blocked, th
may become confused and respond by freezing temporarily: the
most fundamental response to any threat.

Several hunters commented on the apparent altitu
consciousness of chukar after greenup. In covering good terrain
the outset of a hunt, they automatically explored different altitude
When they encountered the first covey of the day, these hunte
continued to hunt at the same approximate altitude until a lack
success indicated to them that the birds had moved higher or lowe
Some hunters actually carried altimeters while hunting in order

able to track altitude as closely as possible. This sensitivity to titude may be related to the presence of fresh grass shoots which e critically dependent upon both moisture and soil temperature for owth. Thus, birds forage from their roosts down to that altitude here they first encounter sufficient soil warmth and moisture to oduce fresh green shoots, and they remain there to feed.

Given the isolation of the terrain, it is clearly safer to hunt with partner or to inform others where you will be hunting, and when ou intend to return. Most hunt with a single partner and pay close tention to their spacing in order to cover ground as efficiently as ossible. For example, there are many mesas forming the tops of lls in chukar country and an abundance of smaller flats, or ateaus, scattered through this land. These are covered with rocky il, scattered sage and some grasses. In this kind of terrain after eenup, two hunters normally start by positioning themselves proximately two shotgun ranges apart and hunt on top, above the mrock, hiking parallel to the edge. One man hunts close to the op off. This alignment is based on a desire to start high, with the kelihood that roosts exist just above or below rimrock and the xpectation that birds may be feeding on top in the vicinity of the ost.

Since birds will flush toward the edge and downhill, the man osest to the drop off walks ahead of his partner in order to obtain assing shots at birds put up by that partner. When this happens the unter at the drop off should kneel or stand still. Flushed chukar ill ignore you if you don't move and will reward you with some allenging pass shooting. These shots are difficult because chukar proach the lip at full speed. Complicating the situation is the cessity for the hunter at the dropoff to do many things at once: ke his shots, mark down birds hit and note the direction taken by eeing birds. The hunter farthest from the rim will get shots only the birds he flushes, while the man adjacent to the rim will have ances at birds he puts up as well as those flushed by his partner; erefore, occasional changes of position are appropriate. It is worth e effort to get right to the edge in an attempt to mark the departing rds' landing area as accurately as possible. They usually fly far ough around the hillside to conceal this from you, but exceptions do occur.

If one man hunts on top while the other hunts below the rir the higher hunter should lag behind the lower man. This imposes bit of a hardship on the top man because his walking conditions a much kinder. He must force himself to move slowly and to go the edge frequently in order to monitor the location of his partne

This sounds pretty simple to execute; however, several facto are likely to complicate things. First, you are not going to t hunting a long, smooth, open hillside where you can easily kee track of each other, because you know that chukar will hear yc and see you there. So the slope you travel will be irregular ar steep. This means that the top man not only traverses smooth terrain but also walks a much shorter distance. Chukar hunters a generally fit and eager. They find it difficult to retard their pace maintain spacing, particularly if likely cover is on the horizo Second, since hunters are frequently out of sight of each othe some form of audible communication must occur periodically. Th means more noise and that's not good.

Finally, your dogs will lead you out of alignment. If Fic clearly becomes birdy, the hunter will follow him to the birds. N problem. But what about all those times when he looks sort birdy? There are few experiences in bird hunting more painful tha failing to honor your dog's birdiness, then watching him flush bir out of range. So you follow him every time he shows enthusiasr sometimes it's a mouse, sometimes it's a meadowlark ar sometimes it's a chukar; but each time, you are led out of alignme with your partner. Consequently, hunting chukar with one or mo partners usually requires a certain amount of self-sacrifice, and may be less productive for the individual than hunting alone.

When both hunters are walking the side of the hill, belo rimrock, they usually space themselves to avoid an overlap of the dogs' hunting ranges, and they try to pursue parallel routes. Whi there is no absolutely correct procedure in this case, I prefer to ha the uphill man continue to lag those below him simply because, most instances, birds will flush down and away from a approaching hunter.

Wind modifies all of these spacings. Chukar use both altitu

nd wind in escaping, so you must adjust to the latter. For example, you are hunting into a stiff breeze the lower man should move vel with the hunter above him. He is anticipating that birds ushing above him will turn with the wind in their attempt to scape, and he isn't eager to find himself in his partner's potential eld of fire.

After flushing a covey, work over the area looking for ragglers, particularly if they don't rise in unison. Young, early eason birds tend to flush a few birds at a time and are more likely o leave some of their kin behind for you. If some are found, note hether the birds utter a call when they rise. John Sullivan notes at, 75 percent of the time, the last remaining bird in a covey will all when flushed. So, if you put up a silent single or two keep oking, the odds favor the presence of more birds nearby.

The majority of birds that escape after being flushed will fly ownhill and curve around the hillside to land out of sight. They sually fly a good distance, but sometimes travel less than a

wo hunters working a hillside are appropriately spaced. The downhill nan is well ahead of his partner and separated from him by pproximately two shot lengths.

hundred yards, particularly in very rugged terrain. They seer satisfied to fly just far enough to be out of sight. The more stresse they are the further they will fly (20), so it's a good idea to hol your fire if you can't manage a good shot. It is certainly true that futile shot at fleeing birds will not induce them to land closer t you.

If you do choose to pursue the broken covey, don't follow th apparent flight path of the disappearing birds, i.e., descend to th spot where they were lost from view. Because, out of sight, the continue their curved flight until they head uphill, land and ru uphill to regroup and find shelter. Therefore, continue to hunt at th altitude at which you flushed the covey and listen for their rall call. When you have traveled a distance greater than that covere by the birds at the time of their disappearance, start to descen obliquely and work down gradually on the birds, listening for ther and trying to analyze their likely location.

It is important to search the patch of cover from which th covey flushed in search of stragglers; however, if you have a goo line on the birds that escaped, don't dawdle in your pursuit. Afte landing, the scattered chukar attempt to regroup and regrouping not in your best interest. You want to find that broken covey i singles and doubles holding tight for you. The tendency of an covey to flush is determined primarily by the spookiest bird in th group. It follows that the more birds there are in the covey, th more likely it is that a nervous bird will be included, and it is th Nervous Nellie that will induce the covey to flush out of rang when you approach it again.

It is generally agreed that birds from a broken covey hold mor tightly than the original covey, so it is worth your while to trac down these birds. In this effort you are largely dependent upon you dog's abilities. If you do find the birds, but fail to shoot them, don waste energy trying to locate them a third time. They will hav flown a long way and will be impossibly spooky.

8

DOGS

Let's return to our hypothetical hunter. He has had a decent ights rest and he has done some scouting and knows of general reas which contain birds. It is time to put his young dog into the ield. A dog is indispensable to chukar hunting. It is difficult to find oveys without a dog, and it is practically impossible to retrieve ead or wounded birds without one. During early days of chukar unting when I was at a distance from my hunting partners, or fflicted with a malfunctioning dog, I found that it was almost npossible to spot a dead chukar on the open ground in typical hukar terrain. The slate gray and brown coloring of the back and pper aspects of wings blends perfectly with the hues of the soil nd rocks.

And you cannot find a wounded bird without a dog. Even with good dog it is frequently difficult. The wounded chukar goes own primarily because of a wing injury; this doesn't impair his unning ability. If it drops in rocky and brushy terrain it will often ide in rocky recesses beneath the dense brush which the dog annot reach. This is where a good dog, one with an excellent nose, ays for himself. I carry leather gloves which help me remove rush in these situations. If the wounded chukar lands in more open over, it is off to the races; you must get your pup on the site as uickly as possible.

The presence of a dog adds enormously to the pleasure of the unt. The dog is actually the focus of the hunt for many hunters. Months and years have been spent in training the dog with both articipants learning to recognize and accept each others' abilities as well as shortcomings. In the field, we spend some time talkir to our partners. More time is spent gazing at the natural worl around us, but most of our attention is focused on the dog and i performance. We know our dogs well and recognize the differenc between birdiness and boredom. When the tail starts to twitch, tl steady searching gait becomes a crouching creep or the dog goes c point, our adrenalin flows, the chest tightens and we prepare for clatter of wings and high pitched squeals.

I have owned Labrador retrievers, and I have not found them 1 be particularly gifted chukar hunters. However, for someor unwilling to train and care for more than one dog at a time, the la has proven an acceptable compromise. My current lab, Pepi, is a excellent retriever of all species of birds, always exhibits hig spirits and she requires little maintenance. I have hunted with oth labs, Brittanys, German shorthairs and one notorious Pudelpoint and I am not a hunting dog expert. It is clear to me, nonetheles that a well trained dog that will point is the companion you want fc hunting chukar.

Kate and Zack, two of John Sullivan's German Shorthaired Pointers o point high above a river in eastern Oregon. Photo by John Sullivan.

Flushing dogs like Pepi hold closer to the hunter than a roaming pointer and cover less ground. This is partially a function of my training her to stay in for hunting quail, but it is also an inbred trait in labs. Remaining nearby sounds like a virtue. After all, isn't it likely that she will flush birds within range of my gun? The answer is no, because when she first scents birds they are usually out of my range, so when she takes off after them, I have to hurry after her to get a shot at the covey. It is exciting when that happens, but I can't keep up with her and given the nature of the ground we are usually traveling, a serious attempt to do so entails risk to ankles and other precious bodily parts. Consequently, I may fail to get a shot at coveys she flushes, and I have to hope that my hunting partners are favorably positioned to benefit from her efforts. Obviously, I still may benefit from a distant flush if I can mark down the fleeing covey and work up scattered birds. On the other hand, when Charlie, my hunting partner Roger's pudelpointer, goes on point or starts her birdy creep, we have time to reposition and we get even more excited.

My opinions are not universally shared, and the subject of dog breed selection is one of continuous debate. Different breeds do possess relatively unique attributes: English Pointers and Setters specialize in scenting and pointing upland birds, while Labrador, Golden and Chesapeake retrievers are expert at finding and retrieving waterfowl. Spaniels, like the Springer Spaniel, are classified as flushing dogs and, like the retrievers, have been bred to take directions well. Many of these dogs can be trained to perform duties well beyond their standard job descriptions. For example, labs will readily learn to flush and retrieve upland birds. My lab occasionally points a bird briefly before flushing it, and this trait has been developed in some to such a degree that a breed of Laboradors now exists that will consistently point upland birds.

Versatile Hunting Dogs were developed in an attempt to combine many of these talents in a single dog. This breed is comprised of German Shorthaired Pointers, Brittany Spaniels, Wiemaraners, Pudelpointers, German Longhairs and others. The dogs have the capacity to scent, point, track and retrieve upland birds and waterfowl. That is a rather high order of expectations for

*Kate, Zack and Ruby all holding steady while a young hunte
approaches. Photo by John Sullivan.*

a single dog, so it is no surprise that individual dogs exhibit mor
aptitude for certain skills than for others.

Perhaps the most important of these aptitudes is the ability t
point steadily and consistently. Some of these dogs will exhibit th
trait as puppies, some will develop it as they mature and some nev
will point. If a puppy, still in the litter, points when tested, you ca
be certain that you are purchasing a pointer. If it does not point, th
breeder may cite this as not unusual for his litters and predict tha
the dog will learn to point with maturity and training. If not, the
will often undertake to train the dog for you, or to exchange it fc
another. Of course, by the time it is apparent that the dog won
point, the owner is often too fond of the dog to part with i
therefore, some experts at training hunting dogs won't take a pupp
that doesn't point while still in the litter (21).

Surprisingly, there are almost as many different hunting styl
as there are breeds of dogs. John Sullivan is 55 years old and retire
a few years ago concluding his career as a high school teacher. H
lives on five acres of fenced land a short distance northeast c
Redmond in central Oregon. He was a triathlete in his younger day

d still runs five miles every day. He has had extensive experience training pointing dogs and has entered them in field trials...with ccess. He is five feet nine inches tall, slim and positively radiates ergetic good will and enthusiasm. He houses his three German orthaired Pointers in a spacious kennel adjacent to his home and eases them twice a day to run around the perimeter of his mpound. He takes the dogs to adjacent BLM property where he ins and exercises them every day.

John sees a chukar hunt as a contest: he and his dogs versus the ukar covey. He aims to take not more than a single bird from ch covey encountered, and he never pursues flushed birds. If he ts his bird, he feels that he and the dogs won that encounter. If ey put up a covey and he fails to get a bird, well and good. The ds won that round; he moves on to find another covey. He hunts ne or with a single dogless guest. He has hunted 40 days or more ery year since he started hunting chukar in 1981 and regularly errupts his hunting to fish for steelhead. He hunts with all three ite bodied German Shorthaired Pointers (two of which are AKC eld Champions) in the field at the same time and encourages them roam widely. When one goes on point, the other dogs honor the int. If the birds start to creep away, he permits the dogs to follow em, and he runs to catch up. His dogs won't approach closer than enty yards from the birds. As a result, he gets a shot at 95 percent the coveys the dogs encounter. He believes that the birds are nerally unaware of the dogs' presence and that his success is gely attributable to the dog's ability to remain in touch, yet at a n-threatening distance from the covey. He is in such superb ysical condition that hunters who know him recognize him in the ld, at long distances by the incredible pace he maintains while ving uphill. Finally, to completely ruin your day, I must add that also carries a two liter bota bag filled with water for each dog.

Bob Hearth is six feet tall, slim and healthy. He is in his early ties, lives in Medford, Oregon, and retired recently. He has nted chukar in eastern Oregon and Nevada since 1962. Despite pressures of work, he managed to take three week-long trips to nt chukar each year. Until recently, he camped in a tent and casionally used a motorcycle with a box on the back for his

Brittany. Not to hunt, but to move from one area to another country too tough for his pickup truck.

He hunts alone or with one companion who also has a dog. believes chukar hold poorly for dogs although singles and doubl from broken coveys hold better. When he approaches patches ground that he feels are likely to hold birds, he keeps the dog close. But he is generally content to have his dog roam at a visible distance. He believes that if the dog flushes a covey out range, it wasn't likely that he could have gotten close enough fo shot, anyway. If he can mark their flight he may pick up sing from the covey later. His Brittany points birds but doesn't hold t point consistently, and given time, eventually flushes the birds that Bob is often forced to run to the point if he is to get a shot. spends more time carefully analyzing the terrain for birdy cov than most hunters interviewed. Therefore, he flushes a number coveys himself. He thinks that the most important functi performed by his dog is the retrieval of downed birds.

At times, his dog has trouble picking up the scent of a wound

Ginger, Rick Schaefer's German Shorthaired Pointer, pointing a fugiti from a covey we had encountered minutes earlier in deep sage.

ıukar. When this occurs he usually attributes it to poor scenting ɔnditions caused by hot, dry, windless, dusty weather. In these ɾcumstances the dog is also breathing hard through its mouth, so ɂ stops hunting, waters the dog and rests it until it is breathing ɔrmally. Then he resumes the search for the wounded bird.

Dave Marsh lived in Bend, Oregon. He passed away not long ter our conversation. He retired after a 30-year career as president ∶ the Mount Bachelor Corporation and resided in a wooded area ı the bank of the Deschutes River, adjacent to a large tract of ɔmmunity property where he jogged and exercised his German ıorthaired Pointers. He hunted chukar for thirty years, and during ost of the last 20 years, he had managed to hunt parts of Nevada, ʹashington, Idaho and Oregon annually. He also hunted mountain ıail and blue and ruffed grouse in the fall, and then migrated to rizona in winter to pursue Gambels quail.

He was tall and sinewy. He too hunted with several dogs; ;ually three, but as many as five simultaneously. He had extensive ɯperience as a dog trainer, trained all of his own dogs and trained

ʹck and Justin O'Toole approach the pointing Ginger in good ignment for the anticipated downhill flush.

dogs for friends as well. Like John Sullivan's dogs, Dave Marsh
German Shorthairs are relatively small, with predominantly whi
bodies and brown heads. They are readily visible in chukar terrai
and he let them roam widely to find birds...as many as 500 cove
in a year. He usually hunted alone because he enjoyed solitude, ai
he found that others had a difficult time maintaining the rapid pa
required in monitoring his dogs.

His dogs honored each other's points at distances up to 1(
yards, and they were encouraged to creep if the birds started
move away. He had seen his dogs creep on a covey of chukar f
one and one half miles without spooking them, and he said that tl
birds would hold for his dogs 95 percent of the time. He said th
his dogs were excellent retrievers, and that he hadn't been forced
break one to retrieve in more than fifteen years. He believed th
the chukar knew that the dogs were there, but that they tolerat
their presence if not approached too closely. If he was slow to con
up on a dog while it was creeping after moving birds, another of h
dogs might circle the covey to cut them off.

John Crafton is 44 years old, about 6 feet 4 inches tall and giv
an impression of great physical strength. He is humorous, open ai
knowledgeable. He grew up on a ranch above the John Day river
north-central Oregon and has hunted chukar since he was six yea
old. He hunts deer and elk early in the year but works full time,
that he usually begins his chukar hunting late in the year, oft
hunting in the snow. He hunts with two Brittanys which l
describes as good "inside" dogs; well behaved with his sma
children. He would prefer to hunt with German Shorthair
Pointers but feels that their high energy levels make them le
suitable as pets in the house and for his family.

In the field, he lets his dogs roam freely and estimates that '
percent of coveys hold for them. Since he frequently hunts in sno
he can often see the chukar when his dogs go on point. When th
happens, he has often observed that the chukar do go on the ale
but hold for the dog if not approached too closely. When the bir
see John, they run or flush immediately.

Doctor William Ellis is a retired Urologist living in Ben
Oregon. He is of average height and build. He doesn't hunt chuk

Good pointing dogs are extraordinary. They scent the birds, point them out to the hunter, find them after they are shot and then deliver them to hand.

early in the year, partly because he feels the young birds are too vulnerable, but also because he enjoys hunting elk and pheasant. He owns three English Setters now and has owned thirteen of these dogs during his hunting career. He considers them excellent hunters with good stamina, and they are good companions for his family. He generally hunts alone or with one guest, and, although he takes all three dogs into the field with him, he hunts them one at a time. He says that his dogs are capable of picking up scent at 100 yards, and that early in the year, 70-80 percent of coveys hold for his dog; this number drops as the season progresses. He agrees that birds will tolerate dogs if not approached too closely, and says that one of his dogs will actually break point and return to heel if the dog gets close enough to see the birds it is pointing.

Steve Leonard is a stocky man of average height. He lives near Prineville in central Oregon and works for the Oregon Bureau of Land Management. He has hunted chukar in western Colorado, Nevada and Oregon since the mid-seventies. He usually hunts with a friend, and he hunts with two Brittanys unless the terrain is very rough, in which case he alternates them. He says that the Brittany

Some days you find the birds, and you shoot straight. Photo by John Sullivan.

is a good family dog, is responsive to commands and has an amiable personality. He lets his dogs roam, and he finds that chukar hold much better for the dogs when the dogs are above them. When he sees his dogs creeping toward a covey and he cannot catch up with them quickly, he sometimes uses a hawk call and has found it effective in freezing the chukar about half the time. He hunts with a double barreled, side-by-side, black powder muzzle loader which he built himself.

It was interesting to note that no hunter interviewed possessed both a retriever and a pointer, even though most of them hunted both waterfowl and upland game. There are probably many explanations for this, but the most apparent one is that each hunter appeared to develop an affection for a certain breed and then stayed with it.

It seems apparent from the observations of these hunters that a minor adjustment in our chukar hunting terminology may be in order. One commonly hears a hunter say that a certain dog "held" the birds, so that he was able to approach them and get a good shot.

And some days you don't. Rick and Phil wryly display the results of an unproductive morning's hunt.

A raptor in the air over birds holds chukar. They freeze in place and do not move until the threat passes. It is also probably true that when a fast moving, far ranging dog like an English Pointer comes abruptly into contact with a covey, the birds may be startled into freezing in a similar fashion (22). For most pointing dogs, however it is probably inaccurate to say that they "hold" the chukar. This term implies that the dogs exert some control over the birds. It is more likely true that birds tolerate the presence of the dog, at an acceptable distance. This is not surprising. It is a response probably conditioned by contact with the other animals routinely encountered in their environment: deer, jackrabbits and cattle; none of which pose a threat to chukar.

The subject of scent merits comment. No hunter knew what constituted the chukar's scent, although Dave Marsh indicated that his dogs had been able to track coveys when they had a trail of fresh stool to follow. I gained no information on the subject by looking through my books and Internet sources. Therefore, the next

Big, strong Labradors are not well suited to long chukar hunts in hot weather, so Rita won't flush any more coveys on this day, but she will find and retrieve every bird shot by Phil and Rick.

me I visited Portland, I went to Powell Books, a famous ookseller noted for their extensive collections of new and used ooks. I looked through every book on the shelves dealing with pland game birds, bird hunting or game dog training. All discussed cent and its importance at length, yet not one described its source r composition. The result of my endeavors was summed up in this entence written by Bill Tarrant, author of many books dealing with ame dog training: "From my work with fox hunters I can admit ere's not a man today who knows one thing about scent" (23).

I saw that national magazines dealing with bird dogs advertised uail and grouse scents as training aids. When I contacted the nanufacturers of the product, I was informed that the only ubstance in the mix from the bird was blood. Blood may be nportant for the dog tracking a wounded bird, but surely it is not e source of the scent which is detected by dogs 100 yards ownwind of an undisturbed covey.

fter five seasons, I'm pretty sure that my Pepi has the message, a but still worry. Every hunter with a young, aggressive dog must bear in ind that dogs are killed or crippled every year while in hot pursuit of ounded chukar fluttering off precipices.

So I don't know what constitutes scent in chukar. I do know that it isn't urine. Chukar produce no liquid urine. All of their urinary excretion exists in the form of uric acid which comprise that white material on the blunt end of their stool. Perhaps scent i derived from more than one source. Fresh stool, blood and som substance associated with skin or feathers may all be importar depending on prevailing conditions. Certainly it is true that som molecule is wafted through the air for distances up to hundreds c yards, and is appreciated as unique to birds by an attentive dog Whatever scent may be, its detection depends on the receptivenes of the dog. All bird dog owners recognize that their dogs have goo days and bad days, and this is one of the best reasons for ownin more than one. Detection of birds also depends on the quality c scenting conditions. While it is always preferable to hunt into th wind we can't always control this element, particularly in th rugged, irregular, hilly terrain which characterizes chukar country Experienced pointing dog handlers observe that chukar coveys ar most likely to flush prematurely when the wind is behind thei dogs, because they must approach the birds more closely to pick u the scent under these conditions.

There is a possibility that chukar possess relatively little scen and that they generate varying amounts of scent in differer conditions. I have been frustrated on several occasions by our dogs inability to pick up the scent of a freshly wounded bird. We hav occasionally put three good dogs into a spot where a bird wa clearly seen to fall, only to see them all express total indifferenc My friend, Paul Foster, is a respected trainer of Labrador Retriever here in the Rogue Valley. He tells me that 25 years ago, the Rogu Valley Retriever Club members became a bit restive about the bill they were paying for the live pheasants used in their field trial. They tried to substitute chukar for the pheasant, since they wer much less expensive. They were forced to abandon the plan whe few of the dogs could find the chukar despite attempts to familiariz the dogs with the new birds. He speculated that chukar may simpl possess less scent than pheasant. He suggested that when a bir was down and crippled, it may be wise to keep hunters out of th

mmediate area, so that their scent doesn't mask the faint scent left
y the bird.

9

HUNTER INTERVIEWS

Certain miscellaneous topics discussed with expert hunters
n't seem to fit conveniently into the text and are presented in this
apter.

What shotgun and shotshell loads do you use? Most hunters
e 12 gauge shotguns with #71/2 lead shot early in the year and #6
ot later in the season. One hunter interviewed shoots a 28 gauge,
de-by-side double which attests to his accuracy. Another uses the
memade percussion cap muzzle loader mentioned earlier, which
a reflection of his strength as well as his sportsmanship. Primary
nsiderations in selection of the shotgun include its weight and its
liability. Half the hunters used double barreled guns and half used
mps or automatic shotguns. When the latter malfunction two
urs into the hunt, precious hunting time is lost in time-consuming
pairs and the problem may not be reparable at all. So the double
rreled weapon has the edge in reliability, but in using one you
rego a third shot.

There exists an ongoing and unresolvable debate between
vocates of double barreled guns, and the pump and automatic
owd, concerning the value of a third shot. The former group
ntend that two shots are maximally efficient when a covey is
shed. They argue that the availability of a third shot induces a
nter to hurry the first shot, in an effort to use all three shells on
e rising birds, and that cleanly killing three birds is beyond the
pability of most hunters. They say that the result is more crippled

birds and failed retrieves, particularly if more than one hunter shooting. I agree as I am rarely able to shoot more than twice at flushing covey. However, I must confess that I don't hit every bir I shoot at, and I am occasionally delighted to have a thir opportunity.

I hunt with a 12 gauge pump. I don't appreciate its weight b the end of the day, but I consider the weight advantage of highe gauge guns insufficient to justify abandoning a weapon whic provides a maximum pattern, particularly when chukar flush at lon range at the end of a long climb. Then there is the issue of the slin A sling provides some relief from the weight of the gun and I hav tried using one. Unfortunately, it slows my reaction time whe birds flush unexpectedly, and it is often an encumbrance when attempt to bring the weapon to my shoulder. It probably shouldn bother me, but it does seem to interfere with my aim, so I don't us one. However, if my dog were a first rate pointing dog and I ha more time to prepare for my shots, I'd be inclined to try the slin again.

Do you hunt chukar with others? Those hunters most focuse on their dogs were more likely to hunt alone. They spent man hours and great energy training and conditioning the dogs and wer devoted to them. Although they occasionally invited a friend t accompany them, it was clear that managing several dogs in th field, keeping pace with them and approaching the flush properl were sufficient to fully occupy them. Serving as a guide for frienc probably proved difficult under these demanding conditions.

Even those hunters with single dogs and those traveling an camping with friends or family, admitted to an inclination to hur alone. Various excuses for this apparently anti-social tendency wer put forth, e.g., "Others can't keep up", but, when pressed, mo confessed to loving the solitude of the hunt and the sense that the were able to overcome harsh conditions and difficult obstacles t achieve success. This attitude did not seem to change as the hunte aged.

Do you hunt the same general areas from year to year? Yes,
they all hunted some of the areas hunted in previous years, but
every one of them indicated that they were constantly looking for
new spots to hunt. "I just like to see new country" was a constant
refrain. As experienced hunters, they most often sought new areas
by poring over topographical maps and integrating that data with
insights accumulated in hunting for many years through several of
the Western States.

One hunter scouted water holes in September in order to
estimate the population of chukar near his home. Others had
scouted prior to the opening of the season in their early years, but
no longer felt it necessary. They said that their experience sufficed
to make them adept at selecting productive chukar terrain. "I scout
by hunting it."

Do you worry about rattlesnakes? All hunters were concerned
about the danger posed to their dogs by rattlesnakes early in the
season. Two hunters totally avoided hunting prior to a good frost
for this reason. It is generally accepted by upland bird hunters that
rattlesnakes will be in hibernation after the first frost. One hunter
sought out a rattlesnake each fall in order to teach his dogs
avoidance but most just took their chances. Only one hunter
interviewed had had a dog bitten by a rattlesnake. His Brittany was
struck on the forepaw while hunting and the snake was immediately
identified and killed. The dog experienced great pain. The puncture
wounds were readily identified and a suction apparatus from a
commercially available snake bite kit was applied. It was
considered effective at removing some of the bloody fluid from the
wound. The dog was seen by a veterinarian the following day and
local wound care was administered. Antivenin was not available
and was not considered necessary. The dog's leg remained swollen
for two days, the wound drained for 10 days and he made a
complete recovery.

This case is typical of rattlesnake bites in hunting dogs.
Although the toxicity of venom varies from snake to snake, even
among snakes of the same species, the outcome of the bite is
primarily dependent upon the location of the bite(s), the size of the

victim and the amount of venom injected. Bites to the face, neck ⟨
trunk are more serious than those inflicted on an extremity. Th
amount of venom injected is primarily a function of the number ⟨
bites inflicted, since rattlesnakes rarely empty their venom sa⟨
during a single strike. Interestingly, in humans, pit viper bit⟨
(rattlesnakes, water moccasins, copperheads) result in ⟨
envenomation at all approximately 20 percent of the time.

Dogs used in hunting chukar are of average to large size. The
are usually moving and are struck when a paw is placed in ⟨
unfortunate location. Responding to the snake's attack and th
immediate, severe pain of a rattlesnake bite, they vacate th
premises instantly. Consequently, they invariably sustain a sing
bite on an extremity and don't receive a large volume of venor
The veterinarians I have spoken with on this subject contrast th
hunting dogs' experience with that of smaller dogs receivir
multiple bite wounds. The Daschund, for example, is at high ris
It is a small dog with a ratter's genetic code: it may stand and fig
the snake, receiving multiple bites to the face and neck which cau:
its death.

Currently, it is unclear for both man and animals, wheth⟨
attempts to remove venom from the site of the wound is appropria
or effective. We are advised to transport the dog promptly to
veterinarian without applying ice or a tourniquet. Bring the de⟨
snake, but be careful handling it since apparently dead snak⟨
sometimes retain a reflex striking capability. Be aware that sma
rattlesnakes may possess venom that is more toxic than veno⟨
found in larger specimens. Rattlesnakes may also lose their rattle
resulting in misidentification of this poisonous snake. Veterinaria⟨
don't routinely stock antivenin because poisonous snake bites a⟨
uncommon, the antivenin has a short shelf life and it is ve⟨
expensive.

At what time of day do you start hunting? Why? There w⟨
great diversity in the responses to this question. The basic messag
was that there is no compelling reason to hunt at any particular tin
of day. Several hunters started hunting at dawn. They said th
concern for dogs in the heat of the early season prompted thi

Others felt that scenting conditions were best in the early hours of the day. When pressed, most acknowledged that they were also early risers, up and eager to get going at dawn. A second group indicated that birds seemed to be most active around 9:30 am. They are away from their roosts, feeding and watering by this hour. Others paid no attention to the time of day. One hunter never starts hunting until after 2 p.m., claiming that birds are farthest from their ankle-threatening roosts in mid-afternoon and more accessible.

Most hunters made no particular effort to spot sentinel birds. One made the point that you will only see them when perched on rocks, not in the open or in sage. Two carried small field binoculars, occasionally scanned for sentinels, but didn't find them particularly effective and used the glasses primarily for sight-seeing.

For all we like to talk about standing at the top of mountains and gazing in rapture at majestic landscapes, the truth is that 99 percent of the time we are hunting, and when you hunt chukar, you watch the ground or risk a broken ankle. Since the prevailing soil is rocky, dry and windswept, tracks are not routinely encountered, but when found, particularly in dusty trails and in muddy water seeps, they are proof that birds are in the area. That certainty always gives a boost to the spirits of the weary hunter. I wondered if the opposite were true, i.e., absence of tracks in decent soil would discourage experienced hunters. Therefore, hunters were asked *If you come across an isolated water hole with water remaining, and good mud fringe, but no tracks, do you quit the area?* Some said they would leave, some said that they wouldn't bother to look because they were guided entirely by their dogs but one got the grand prize. He pointed out that a good mud fringe would cause drinking birds to feel exposed to predators. Accordingly, he would walk downhill from the pool to seek a seep emerging from the ground where birds could drink in the protecting cover of surrounding brush.

Does finding chukar stool help in finding the birds? Can you age the stool? Most hunters felt that only fresh stool was helpful and then it was primarily a morale booster since it indicated tha birds had been in the vicinity recently. Two of the hunters trie using fresh stool as scent for their dogs. One was unsuccessful, an the other said that his dogs had been able to follow really fresh stoc directly to birds on more than one occasion.

A basic understanding of the chukar's digestive processes wi help you to identify fresh droppings. Food is temporarily stored i the bird's crop, then ground up with the aid of small bits of grave in the muscular gizzard, a component of the stomach. Nutrients ar absorbed in the small intestine while waste is passed along an stored in the cloaca until evacuated through the bird's vent onto th ground. The cloaca is a combined rectum and urinary bladder.

Fresh chukar stool has the shape of a slightly tapered cylinde about one inch long. It is green and moist with a white cap at th larger end. The green hue is derived from the fresh greens in th diet, and the white cap is composed primarily of uric acid excrete as urine. On the ground, in time and with exposure to the elemen the uric acid dissolves and disappears, the green color fades to ligl tan and the margins of the cylinder become ragged. A bir consuming a diet of seeds and roots early in the season passes stool which is brown; therefore, it cannot be distinguished, b color, from the aging stool of a bird which dined on greens. So te: it for moisture. Once a fresh stool loses its moisture, it remains dr and will not reabsorb dew or rainfall because it is composed of fibr and other water repellent materials. This is why chukar dropping may remain intact for months or years on undisturbed ground.

On three occasions I have flushed a single bird seemingl beyond the range of birds encountered earlier in the day. I hav wondered whether they were simply chukar separated from the covey or sentinel birds. If the latter, it would imply that I ha missed the covey. So I asked: *You are hunting in the middle c nondescript territory and you encounter a single chukar. How ofte have you found a covey nearby?* Because they did not find covey in the area, most hunters considered that such singles wer relatively young birds separated from broken coveys, not sentinel

Is it important to hunt south facing slopes in cold weather? All ;reed that chukar seek south facing slopes in cold weather and that e relatively large numbers of birds flushed in these locations dicated that coveys were flocking once again. During our discussion, two hunters spontaneously volunteered eir impression that, over a period of many years, East-facing rrain seemed to produce the largest numbers of chukar. hristianson made the same observation in 1970 (4), and indbloom (11) and Walter (12) provided support for this)servation when they routinely recorded compass headings for 1ukar nests, coveys and individual bird locations. For example, indbloom found that 87 percent of chukar nests were located on opes with a southeast aspect, and both investigators noted that the 1ukar's favorite foods and type of ground cover existed in greatest)undance on southeast facing slopes.

These observations suggest that the prudent chukar hunter will 1rry a compass.

If your dog flushes a covey out of range, and you can observe : which direction they are headed as they disappear from view, 1ould you go to the location of the flush, seeking stragglers, or 1rsue the fleeing covey? A key to this query lies in estimating the kelihood that stragglers remain at the site of the flush. The odds .vor the presence of stragglers when the covey rises in a gradual, sorganized manner. This type of rise is typically seen earlier in e year when many young birds are present. They have not been ·essured, and are clearly disinclined to fly. In contrast, later in the :ason when the covey springs up in unison, there are not likely to : stragglers.

The quality of the terrain, numbers of birds in the covey and)parent distance flown all have bearing on the decision regarding 1rsuit. However, this decision is also predicated on the pattern of ight assumed by the departing birds. If they flee in close formation ey will probably remain together on landing, and they will be)ooky. On the other hand, if they scatter on the flush it is to your lvantage since scattered birds will hold more tightly.

10

PARTING SHOTS

In the course of my interviews with hunters for this book, I
ten enquired about amusing experiences they might have enjoyed
ıring their years of chukar hunting. One man related that he had
ıce literally dragged his dog away from a patch of ground which
e dog had pointed, and which they had worked over thoroughly
ithout finding a bird. When he was 50 yards away, the chukar
ey couldn't find flew off. He thought that was pretty funny and so
d I, but I'm not sure that a non-hunter would see the humor in this
perience.

Ten years ago, several of us parked trailers next to a small
servoir in central Oregon and hunted quail and waterfowl. My
ın, Justin, arrived early one afternoon after a long drive from
ırtland. When he and his girlfriend rejoined us after a short walk
stretch their legs, he commented "Dad, its pretty ironic that
ıu've been driving all over the valley this morning looking for
ıail. A nice covey just walked right by us." When I looked in the
rection he indicated, I saw the unmistakable figures of chukar
ceding in the distant sage. We pursued them without success.

A year ago, Roger Hutchings and I hunted a broken covey of
ıukar by following the birds' tracks in fresh snow. We were 40
rds apart, when a rabbit appeared in front of Roger. It ran directly
him, passed within a few feet and then flew into the air. Roger
ot that rabbit in the air at thirty yards, and to my amazement, on
ɔse inspection it had transformed itself into a chukar. It was
rtunate that Roger's vision was superior to mine. I was totally

unprepared to shoot a flying rabbit.

This year I hunted with Justin and friends in eastern Oregon fo
quail and pheasant. We had been told that there were some chuka
in the area, but we were primarily interested in pheasant since w
hadn't had the opportunity to hunt them for many years. Justin an
I hunted together on the third afternoon along a lovely cree
bordered by rose bushes, heavy brush and trees. Sage covered th
hillsides of our canyon. The dogs had flushed two cocks and man
hen pheasant, all of which flew up along the hillside and into th
sage; therefore, on retracing our route, we worked the sage. We ha
flushed two or three single hen pheasants when another hen aros
quite close to me. As I dutifully held my fire, it crossed the path o
the late afternoon sun to reveal a peculiar pinkish hue on its boc
and it exhibited a unusually erratic flight pattern for a pheasant. M
next utterance "Justin, could that have been a chukar?" was close
followed by the sound of my son shooting the first chukar of th
season.

It is somewhat embarrassing to admit that I confused a chuk
with a pheasant, but the episode makes a point. All the humor
have encountered in chukar hunting is wry humor. It arises from th
misadventures of the hunters. Chukar hunting is not an inherent
amusing activity. Far from it. It is hard physical work guided by
series of educated guesses regarding the birds' whereabouts an
behavior, sometimes rewarded with success.

It is regrettable that anti-hunting sentiment in the United Stat
seems to be gaining strength. The number of game bird hunte
afield in Western states is decreasing. Fewer youngsters apply f
hunting licenses, and each year more attempts to ban the taking
game appear on ballots, in the form of initiatives sponsored by th
public. The reasons for this shift in sentiment are complex, b
certainly include the ongoing migration of our population fro
rural lands to urban centers. Interest in hunting and related pursui
is contingent on some contact with the natural world in childhoc
or adolescence, so it isn't surprising that the percentage
applications for hunting licenses is higher in rural than
metropolitan areas. It isn't hard to understand why individuals, wh
spend their lives in offices or in front of computers, have troub

ing sympathetic to the cause of hunting. But it saddens me that many youngsters will miss out on the excitement, joy and owledge to be gained from hunting wild birds in beautiful untry.

Our best response to this problem lies in continued education the public and in efforts to involve our youth by way of ograms which facilitate their entry into the exciting world of inting. Whether you join a group to participate in this endeavor or nply continue to support it privately, you will eventually be lled upon to justify your sport. Some evening toward the end of dinner party, as you relax among friends and reminiscences of inting seasons past, a voice will address you from the other end the table. The voice will belong to a pleasant and intelligent rson who will ask, in a soft tone which doesn't quite conceal itation, "How can you justify killing those beautiful birds that od created?"

If you aren't ready for this, you're dead. If you lose your mper, you're deader. Justifications such as "I put a lot of time, oney and effort into hunting"– "The flavor of the birds is unique d unobtainable in any other way" – or "My valuable and highly ined dog will be wasted if not hunted" will get you nowhere.

Start your reply by acknowledging the sincerity of your quisitor's concern, since you share his appreciation of the beauty the birds, and you, too, are grateful for this bounty which God s granted us. Mention that hunting concerns are not ethical issues. bate over the merits of hunting is legitimate, but should not be uated to the level of importance associated with issues of ndamental human concern such as poverty, starvation and the eaning of life.

Make it clear that hunting and killing are not synonymous. Yes, ath often occurs during hunting, but it is often tinged with dness or ambivalence and is not the sole focus of the hunt. A hunt composed of many different ingredients: excited anticipation, iborate planning with friends, physical conditioning of the hunter d training of dogs and acquisition of the terrific gear which we ve convinced ourselves will ensure success. It includes the mpanionship of close friends and tightens bonds with offspring in a way that other forms of shared experience cannot. It deepen our understanding and appreciation of our hunting and explorin forefathers.

Hunting birds is a matter of taste, preference and fundament inclination. Its legal pursuit does not call into question the mora of those who hunt. We hunt because we love the challenge an excitement of the sport. Those of us who have inherited th capacity for deriving so much pleasure from this activity understan that we have been blessed with a unique gift. We need not off excuses for pursuing this pleasure as long as it brings no harm others.

Finally, as Lisa Debruyckere has written so eloquently, "Whe you are a hunter, and you have experienced this respect an nurturing for wildlife and habitats, while at the same tim harvesting and caring for your harvest, there is a richness about li and our environment, and a special, personal closeness an belonging to the outdoors that simply cannot be matched. An while I come close to experiencing this same level of connectic when I birdwatch, canoe, hike or camp, these types of experienc fall short when compared to hunting. And the best thing about it that I cannot explain why." (24)

You can't ask for better conditions: a light snowfall at night, clear ski during the day, a gifted Pudelpointer, and a straight shooting hunter

11

HUNTING GEAR

You can't use it if you didn't bring it; therefore, it is extremely :lpful to make a checklist of the gear you might need for hunting ıukar. Scan it every day before you leave camp. No matter how ganized and experienced you are, the day will come when you are shed for some reason, and you will leave an important item in ımp. This is my current list:

Shotgun

Shotshells loaded into a leather shell belt. This is worn just over e hips and reduces the shoulder load.

Whistle.

Ear plugs.

Lip balm.

Sunglasses/glasses.

Toilet paper/facial tissues.

Disposable plastic gloves for cleaning birds (see Chapter 12).

Scissors. Fiskars scissors, available everywhere, are sharper, lighter and a lot cheaper than game shears. (see Chapter 12).

Multipurpose tool (Leatherman, Gerber). This contains an ceptable knife and excellent pliers for extracting improperly :cted shells from my shotgun as well as porcupine quills from the ızzle of my lab.

Calls. Chukar, crow, predator.

Roll of adhesive tape.

Leather gloves for warmth, hand holds on steep inclines and :aring brush

Compass.

GPS Navigator. If you have one of the small hand-held uni
and you have trouble finding your way home. Most of these uni
have an altimeter function if you wish to pursue birds by altituc
after green-up.

Dog leash. For dog protection when near roads.

Cash.

Hunting license and drivers license.

Hat with visor.

Fanny pack. It shifts more weight off shoulders.

Vest or shooting coat with game pouch. Make sure that tl
latter is readily accessible, preferably from a front vent, so that yc
aren't doing a contortionists act putting a freshly killed bird into tl
pouch when that straggling chukar flushes at your feet. Don't pa
extra for those glitzy shell loops. They all become permanent
stretched and lose their shell-carrying capacity. Flapped pocke
must have secure closures, usually velcro.

Camera and film – sometimes.

Collapsible bowl made of fabric. My dog wastes most of tl
water squirted into her mouth from a squeeze bottle.

Water bottles. Water for dog, half strength Gatorade or simil
electrolyte containing drink for you. The dog doesn't sweat; you d
and you may lose significant amounts of sodium and potassiu
which can cause cramping and weakness.

Snacks. For you, perhaps for your dog. Some dogs, lil
humans, lose their appetite for solid food when exercising intensel

Light rain jacket/windbreaker with hood. These can be fou
in golf shops. Carried in your fanny pack, it will save you when tl
wind comes up and the temperature drops unexpectedly.

IN THE RIG

Back-up shotgun.

Binoculars. These are great for scanning the terrain f
mountain goats, deer, etc., but don't add enough to the pursuit
chukar to justify their weight during the hunt.

Change of boots and socks.

5 gallons of water and bowl.

Cooler with ice for preservation of birds and cold drinks. Medical kit. That's right, in the vehicle. Lacerations and rains, the common injuries, can be managed with your roll of tape nd a strip of fabric from the tail of your shirt. Anything more rious can't be addressed properly with the amount of medical ear you can carry while hunting.

Many hunters have adopted the multilayered approach to othing. I wear oversized brush pants with a canvas face. They are fficiently cool for me, but if you want to wear very lightweight ousers on hot days consider carrying nylon chaps. They are light, sily carried in your fanny pack and readily available from most ail order catalogues. On cold days, I wear medium weight olypropylene underwear tops and bottoms. If I overheat, I remove and carry it in my pack. It is so light and compressible that it is ardly noticeable.

I also carry a 16-foot fiberglass, camouflaged canoe on the roof f my vehicle. Inside the rig are the paddles, electric motor, battery, aders and life jacket. There is more than one way to get away om the crowd; when I can avoid a long hike by taking a boat ride, do it.

As a retired physician, I'll restrict myself to a single health tip. uring the early season, at the outset of the hunt, when you apply unscreen to your face, please smear a generous amount on the per and outer margins of your ears. Most hunters wear baseball pe caps which leave the ears exposed, and, despite what they say those ads on the radio, dermatologists *love* sun fried ears.

Happy is the hunter who remembers his latex gloves for gutting birds in the field, far from water on a warm Fall day. Photo by Richard Schaefer.

12

PREPARATION AND PRESERVATION OF GAME

Birds are field dressed promptly after they are retrieved. Chukar ave delicate flesh with a mild game flavor. They are a prized bird or the table, and deserve proper handling in the field. My wife, Mary Ellen, enjoys them so much that she tells me they almost make up for all the ducks she has eaten. Since water is usually not available for flushing the body cavity, pay attention to detail in evacuating the contents of the abdomen. It is important to avoid damaging the gastrointestinal tract and soiling the cavity with stool. On a warm day, soiled birds carried in a vest will ripen quickly.

Start by slicing open the crop to learn what (and perhaps where) they have been eating. Then pluck the feathers from the skin overlying the abdominal cavity from the keel of the breast bone to the vent. Pinch the exposed skin between two fingers, rolling it gently back and forth to separate the skin from any underlying bowel, then lift a small segment of skin and create a 1/4 inch opening with your knife. Insert the tips of your closed scissors just into the hole and extend the incision by spreading the scissor blades apart. Since the backs of the blades are dull this will avoid damage to the gut. Using scissors or fingers (the skin here is easily torn) extend the opening sufficiently to allow you to insert your second and third fingers into the abdominal cavity, up beneath the breast toward the head, with your palm directed toward the bird's spine.

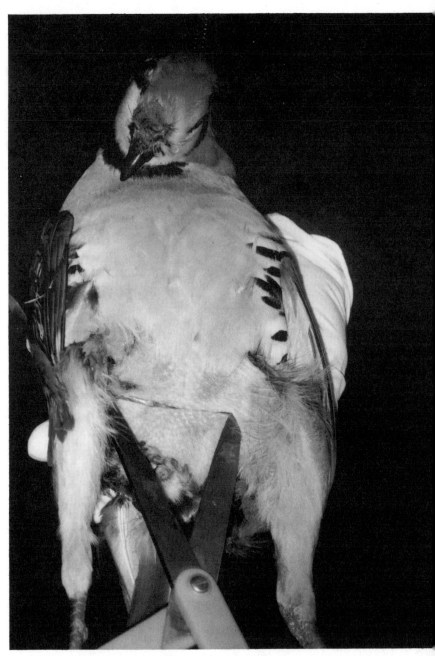

Pluck the feathers from the tip of the breast bone to the vent, then crea
a small opening just below the breast bone with your sharply pointe
knife. Insert the tips of your closed scissors, then spread them apart t
create an opening sufficiently wide to admit your second and thir
fingers.

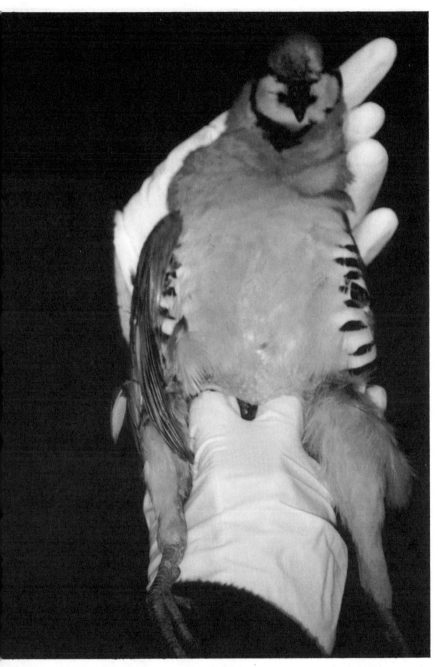

...sert your fingers up behind the breast bone with your palm facing the bird's spine. Reach to the limits of the body cavity, and press firmly through the soft lungs...

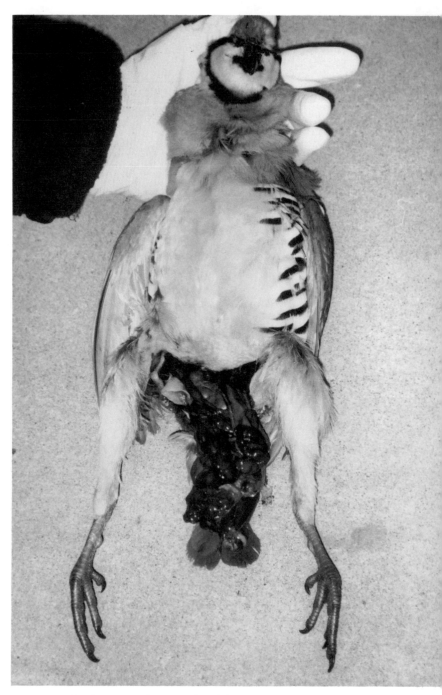

...grasp the heart and gizzard (feels like a chestnut) and remove all th *body cavity contents in one firm movement. They are all now suspende* *from the vent.*

*single scissor cut above the vent and across the lower spine severs all
abdominal contents, tail feathers, and parsons nose.*

The final product.

...he same procedure executed in the field preserves the quality of the ...me while providing a bit of nutrition for scavengers. Photo by Roger ...utchings.

Working fingers carefully past potential bone fragments ...slodged by your shot, reach to the limits of the body cavity where ...ou will encounter the soft, air-filled lungs and the heart. Press ...rmly through this material up against the back of the chest, grasp ...e gizzard firmly and, in a single movement, pull everything out. ...he intestinal tract separates above the gizzard at the esophagus, so ...cal matter is not spilled.

At this juncture, you are holding the eviscerated bird in your ...and with all of the chest and abdominal contents hanging from the ...nt. Cut transversely with your scissors across the lower spine to ...parate the vent, abdominal contents, tail feathers and parsons nose ... a single cut. Now you understand why you carried a serious pair ...f scissors instead of the tiny scissor on the multipurpose tool.

If water is near, flush the blood from the abdominal cavity. ...tuff some dried brush into the cavity to enhance air circulation and ...cilitate cooling of the bird. Congratulate yourself if you ...membered to bring the plastic gloves; otherwise, wipe your ...ngers on whatever is available and resume hunting.

On arriving at my vehicle, I place the birds in the cooler on plastic bottles containing frozen water. When I return to camp, flush out the body cavity with water. Wings and lower legs are the removed with scissors, birds are stored, two at a time, in gallo plastic bags and refrigerated or frozen. Heads are left on to perm identification by state game officials according to law.

The primary aim of game preparation in the field is to avoi bacterial contamination of the meat. The main goal in subseque handling of these birds is to prevent drying of the meat. Therefor on returning home, no further dressing of birds which are destine for recipes calling for whole chukar is attempted. Skin, feathers an heads are left intact, and birds are vacuum packed and froze When it is their turn on the menu, they are thawed, skinned an beheaded. Hard hit birds are filleted so that shot can be remove Note that birds which are vacuum packed must be frozen or d when processed. If moisture is present, the vacuum will suck wat into the area of the heat seal, and the packages will later open in th freezer when this moisture freezes and expands.

There are many other perfectly satisfactory methods preparation. Hunters taking large numbers of chukar often fillet th breasts and remove the thighs of all their birds. Some pluck thos birds which have been little damaged finding that a plucked an stuffed bird makes a particularly attractive presentation at the tabl

Because the chukar's flavor is delicate we prefer simp preparations that don't mask this flavor. Accordingly, the followin recipes are either simple or complex. The latter group contai recipes which add more ingredients and flavor to the bird. Feel fr to adjust amounts of ingredients and to make substitutions. W favor fresh herbs and mushrooms when available. These recip have been developed and adjusted over a period of 30 years, an most are readily applied to other game birds such as quail an pheasant. In the following recipes chukar are whole birds whic have been skinned or plucked unless otherwise specified.

Oven temperatures and the size of birds will vary, so alway test for doneness. Use a meat thermometer (180 degrees) or obta clear fluid when the thigh is pierced. Let's start with a versati sauce and stuffing.

Sharon's Excellent Sauce For Any Upland Game Bird

Soak 1/2 cup raisins in 1/2 cup creme de cassis for 30 minutes. Drain and reserve liquid.

2 cups veal stock (or other)
2 cups evaporated milk
1 tsp fresh lemon juice

In separate pans simmer milk and stock until reduced by half, about 30 minutes. Add creme de cassis to stock and simmer until reduced to 1 cup.

Brown game in butter and salt and pepper on stove top. Remove bird and roast in oven.

Pour stock, reduced milk and lemon sauce into skillet and whisk to incorporate pan drippings. Increase heat and whisk continuously until reduced by half. Add raisins and lemon sauce. Serve over bird. Don't add salt and pepper while cooking sauce because it will curdle.

Howard Davol's Mustard Chukar

Slather the thighs and filleted breasts of chukar in fresh Grey Poupon Dijon mustard. Roll them in crushed Corn Flakes, Saltine crackers or bread crumbs and sautee in equal parts of butter and olive oil. This is our favorite recipe in camp and is superb with upland game or waterfowl.

Stuffing For Any Upland Game Bird

2 cups chopped yellow onion
1 cup chopped celery
6 tbsp butter
8 cups toasted bread cubes
1 cup diced apples
1 cup diced dried apricots
1/2 cup minced fresh parsley
2 tsp minced fresh oregano
1/2-1 cup chicken stock
1 lb sausage (optional)

Saute onions and celery in butter until translucent. If usin
sausage, add to pan and saute 4-5 minutes. Remove from heat.

In a large mixing bowl combine above mixture with remainin
ingredients except stock. Mix thoroughly. Gradually add stock unt
mixture is moist but loose.

Stuff birds for roasting.

Mediterranean Chukar

2 cups cooked rice
3/4 cup chopped fresh spinach
1/4 cup chopped sun-dried tomatoes in oil
2 chukar
2 cloves garlic, minced
2 tbsp melted butter

Add spinach and tomatoes to rice. Spoon into cavity of chukar
Combine garlic and butter. Brush on bird. Roast 45-50 minutes @
425 degrees until juices run clear, basting occasionally with garli
butter.

Elegant Chukar

4 chukar, halved
1/2 cup consomme
3 oz brandy
1-2 cups seedless green grapes
Brown birds in butter. Add consomme. Simmer 10 minutes.
Add brandy, cover and roast @350 degrees for 30 minutes. Add
more liquid if needed then add grapes. Bake for an additional 30
minutes.

Chutney Crust Chukar

2 chukar
1/2 cup Dijon-style mustard
1/2 cup chutney (eg., Major Greys Chutney)
1/4 tsp cumin
1/2 tsp curry powder
Preheat oven to 450 degrees. Place birds in a shallow baking
dish with cover. Combine remaining ingredients in a small bowl.
Spoon sauce over birds leaving thick layer on top. Cover and bake
at 450 degrees for 15 minutes. Reduce heat to 375 degrees and
continue baking uncovered for 30 additional minutes or until done.

Faye And Mary Ellen's Chukar

Stuffing mix: to your taste
Brandied cherries or dried cranberries
Diced onion
Chopped nuts
Dried raisins. currants or dates, chopped
Saute these ingredients in butter and add to stuffing mix with stock to moisten.

Stuff chukar. Place remaining stuffing around chukar in roasting pan. Sprinkle breasts and thighs powdered ginger, dry mustard, tarragon, rosemary and parsley.

Bake at 350 degrees covered with foil tent for 45 minutes or until done.

Optional sauce. Remove birds and stuffing when done. Mix together 2 tbsp flour, 1/2 cup sherry, 2 cups chicken broth and 1/2 cup cream. Add to pan drippings and whisk constantly over medium heat until thickened. Pour over birds and serve.

Roast Chukar With Lemon

2 chukar
Salt and pepper
2 lemons
Sprigs of rosemary
Dry white wine or vermouth
Preheat oven to 350 degrees. Wash bird in cold water, drain and dry. Soften lemon by rolling on counter. Pierce lemon and place in body cavity.

Truss legs. Sprinkle breast with sprigs of rosemary. Splash with wine. Put chukar in roasting pan and roast for 45-60 minutes until done.

Chukar With Cherry-Orange Sauce

2 chukar

Dressing: Brown one small chopped onion in 2 tbsp butter. Add /3 cup diced ham and 1/3 cup diced mushrooms. Saute 5 minutes 1en add and mix well, 3/4 cup cooked wild rice. Stuff chukar with 1is mixture.

Sauce: 4 tsp cornstarch, 4 tbsp sugar, 1/4 tsp salt, 1/4 tsp dry 1ustard and 1/4 tsp ginger. Mix together.

Drain a one pound can of red, sour, pitted cherries water acked. Add cherry liquid to cornstarch mixture with

1 tbsp slivered orange rind

1/2 cup orange juice

1/4 cup currant jelly

Cook over medium heat stirring constantly until mixture boils nd thickens. Add drained cherries and 2 tbsp sherry.

Bake birds in shallow casserole dish at 350 degrees for 45-60 1inutes and baste with butter. When almost done pour sauce over irds.

REFERENCES

1. Report of the 1998 Game Take Survey. California Department of Fish and Game. 1998.

2. Game Harvest Statistics 1999 - 2000. Nevada Division of Wildlife. 2000.

3. 1999 Game Harvest Report. State of Washington Department of Fish and Wildlife. 2000.

4. Christensen, Glen C. *The Chukar Partridge: Its Introduction, Life History and Management.* Nevada Department of Fish and Game Biological Bulletin 4. Reno, 1970.

5. Galbreath, D. S. and Moreland, R. *The Chukar Partridge In Washington.* Washington State Game Department Biological Bulletin 11. 1953.

6. Harper, H.T., Harry, B. H. and Bailey, W. D. " The Chukar Partridge In California." California Fish and Game 44: 5-50. 1958.

7. Masson, Vic. "The Chukar In The Southeast Region." Oregon State Game Commission Bulletin. 14 (6), 3-8. 1959.

8. Sandfort, Wayne. "A Decade Of Chukar Hunting." Colorado Outdoors, Nov/Dec. 1967, 20-23.

9. Bizeau, E. Chukar Partridge in Idaho. Idaho Wildlife Review, Jan-Feb pp3-4, 1962.

10. Johnsgard, Paul A. The Quails, Partridges, and Francolins of the World. Oxford University Press. 1988.

11. Lindbloom, A. Habitat Use, Reproduction, Movements, and Survival of Chukar Partridge in West-Central Idaho. Thesis. University of Idaho, Moscow, Idaho, USA. 1998.

12. Walter, H. Ecology of the Chukar in Eastern Oregon. Thesis. University of Idaho, Moscow, Idaho, USA. 2000.

13. Stuart Love, Wildlife Biologist, Oregon Dept of Fish and Wildlife, Ontario, Or. Personal communication. 2000.

14. Billings, W.D. Vegetational Zonation in the Great Basin of North America, *in* les bases Ecologiques de la regeneration de la vegetation des zones arides. U.I.S.B. 101-122, 1951.

15. Stokes, A.W. Voice and social behavior of the chukar partridge. The Condor 3 (2) 111-127, 1961.

16. Stokes, A.W. Agonistic and sexual behavior in the chukar partridge (Alectoris raeca). Animal Behavior 11 (1) 121-134, 1963.

17. Bohl, W.H. Experiments in locating wild chukar partridges by use of recorded alls. Jour. of Wildlife Management. 20 (1) 83-85, 1956.

18. Williams, H.W. The influence of physical and biological factors on the ral call of the chukar partridge (Alectoris graeca) with regard to use of the call as a censi method. Proc. 41st Conf. West. Assoc. State Game and Fish Comm. 117-129, 1961

19. Williams, H. W. and Stokes, A.W. Factors affecting the incidence of ral calling in the chukar partridge. Condor 67 (1) 31-43, 1965.

20. Christensen, Glen C. Chukar. *in* The Birds of North America. Vol. 7. Pub. I The American Ornithologists Union and The Academy of Natural Sciences. Phil 1977.

21. Mueller, Larry. Speed Train Your Own Bird Dog. Stackpole Books. 1990. p 13 - 18.

22. Waterman, Charles F. Hunting Upland Birds. Countrysport Press. 1997. p 149-173

23. Tarrant, Bill. "Hey Pup, Fetch It Up". Stackpole Books, 1979, 1993.

24. Debruykere, Lisa A. Outdoor Perspectives. *in* Oregon Wildlife. Vol. 56, # pp 22 - 23. 2001.

LISTING OF BOOKS

Additional copies of **HUNTING CHUKAR: A No-Nonsense Guide to the** *uccessful Hunting of The West's Most Elusive Game Bird and many other* * *Stoneydale Press' books on outdoor recreation, big game hunting, or* *storical reminisces centered around the Pacific Northwest and Northern* *ocky Mountain regions, are available at many book stores and sporting goods* *ores, or direct from Stoneydale Press. If you'd like more information, you* *in contact us by calling a Toll Free Number,* **1-800-735-7006,** *by writing the* *ldress at the bottom of the page, or contacting us on the Web at* *ww.stoneydale.com. Here's a partial listing of some of the books that are* *vailable.*

Hunting Books

olving **Elk Hunting Problems,** *by Mike Lapinski. As one of America's most* *dely published and respected elk hunters, Mike Lapinski takes you into great detail* *this book outlining ways to deal with difficult elk hunting situations. 192 pages,* *any photographs, hardcover or softcover.*

igh **Pressure Elk Hunting,** *By Mike Lapinski. The latest book available on* *inting elk that have become educated to the presence of more hunters working them.* *ots of info on hunting these elk.192 pages, many photographs, hardcover or* *ftcover.*

ugling **for Elk,** *By Dwight Schuh, the bible on hunting early-season elk. A* *cognized classic, 164 pages, softcover edition only.*

Hunt For the Great Northern, *By Herb Neils. This acclaimed new novel utilizes* *e drama of a hunting camp as the setting for a novel of intrigue, mystery, adventure* *id great challenge set in the woods of northwestern Montana. 204 pages, softcover.*

host of **The Wilderness,** *By James "Mac" Mackee. A dramatic story of the pursuit* * *the mountain lion, the Ghost of The Wilderness. A tremendous tale of what Jim* *acKee went through over several seasons in his quest for a trophy mountain lion in* *e wilds of Montana. 160 pages, softcover.*

he **Woodsman And His Hatchet,** *By Bud Cheff. Subtitled "Eighty Years on* *ilderness Survival," this book gives you practical, common sense advice on survival* *der emergency conditions in the wilderness. Softcover.*

lemoirs of **An Idaho Elk Hunter,** *By Jens Andersen. This big book captures the* *tality and romance of a lifetime spent hunting elk in Idaho and Montana. A superb* *ad, many color photographs and illustrations. 216 pages, hardcover only.*

oyote **Hunting,** *By Phil Simonski. Presents basics on hunting coyotes as well as* *tring for the pelts, 126 pages, many photographs, softcover only.*

lk **Hunting in the Northern Rockies,** *By Ed Wolff. Uses expertise of five* *cognized elk hunting experts to show the five basic concepts used to hunt elk.* *other of our very popular books, 162 pages, many photographs.*

So You Really Want To Be a Guide, By Dan Cherry. *The latest and single mc* authoritative source on what it takes to be a guide today. This book is an excelle guideline to a successful guiding career. Softcover edition only.

Hunting Open Country Mule Deer, By Dwight Schuh. *Simply the best and mc* detailed book ever done for getting in close to big mule deer. The ultimate mule de book by a recognized master, 14 chapters, 180 pages.

Montana Hunting Guide, By Dale A. Burk, *the most comprehensive and fact-fill* guidebook available on hunting in Montana, 192 pages, clothbound or softcov editions.

Taking Big Bucks, By Ed Wolff. *Subtitled "Solving the Whitetail Riddle, " this bo* presents advice from top whitetail experts with an emphasis on hunting weste whitetails. 176 pages, 62 photographs.

Radical Elk Hunting Strategies, By Mike Lapinski. *Takes over where other boo* on early-season elk hunting leave off to give advice on what the hunter must do adapt to changing conditions. 162 pages, 70 photographs.

Western Hunting Guide, By Mike Lapinski, *the most thorough guide on hunting t* western states available. A listing of where-to-go in the western states alone makes t book a valuable reference tool. 168 pages, softcover.

Books By Duncan Gilchrist

On Caribou Hunting, By Duncan Gilchrist. *This first-ever comprehensive c* caribou hunting was written by a dedicated hunter with almost 40 years of experien on hunting them across their entire range. Provides information and insight on hunti caribou wherever the nonresident is allowed to pursue them. 176 pages, softcover

Quest for Giant Bighorns, By Duncan Gilchrist. *Comprehensive overview c* hunting bighorn sheep everywhere they're hunted; detailed how-to, where-to with lc of photos. 224 pages, softcover.

Quest for Dall Rams, By Duncan Gilchrist. *The best source book ever put togeth* on the beautiful Dall sheep, it's crammed with solid how-to and where-to informati on hunting Dall sheep. 224 pages, 88 photographs, many charts, softcover format

Montana–Land of Giant Rams, Vol. III, By Duncan Gilchrist. *The best sour* and most acclaimed book available on hunting bighorn sheep in Montana. Updat and expanded from his earlier volumes on the same subject. 224 pages, ma photographs, softcover format.

Successful Big Game Hunting, By Duncan Gilchrist. *For more than four decac* now, Duncan Gilchrist has hunted across North America as well as in Africa and Ne Zealand. This book touches every aspect of what it takes to be a successful hunter. 1 pages, 82 photographs, both softcover and hardcover formats.

Field Care Handbook, By Duncan Gilchrist and Bill Sager. *The mc* comprehensive field guide available for the care of big game, birds, fish and oth species. Illustrated by many of Duncan's photographs taken in the field. 168 page many photographs and illustrations, comb binding so it will lay flat while you use

Cookbooks

Camp Cookbook, Featuring Recipes for Fixing Both at Home and in Camp, Wi Field Stories by Dale A. Burk, 216 pages, comb binding.

hat Perfect Batch: The Hows and Whys of Making Sausage and Jerky, By *lem Stechelin. Detailed instruction on techniques of making sausage and jerky at ome from wild game, beef, etc. 116 pages, many photographs, comb binding.*

ooking for Your Hunter, By *Miriam Jones, 180 pages, comb binding.*

ooking on Location, By *Cheri Eby. Exhaustive content for cooking on location in e outdoors, from menu planning to camp organization, meal preparation, and cipes for all sorts and styles of dishes. 139 pages, color photos and illustrations, omb binding.*

enison As You Like It, By *Ned Dobson. A manual on getting the most from game eat, with over 200 recipes and instructions on using a variety of cooking methods. etailed index, softcover.*

Historical Reminisces

ale Burk's MONTANA, By *Dale A. Burk. A lively and incisive text combines ith 150 stunning color photographs in one of the most beautiful books about Montana er published. Issued in large format, full color. Hardcover and softcover editions.*

ule Tracks: The Last of The Story, By *Howard Copenhaver. The master oryteller out of Montana's Bob Marshall Wilderness is at it again in what he says ill be his final book in which he focuses his attention on the often unpredictable and ny antics of the beloved mules with whom he traversed thousands of miles in the ilds of the Bob Marshall Wilderness – plus other stories touched by Howard's warm nse of humor. 176 pages, many photographs. Hardcover or softcover.*

openhaver Country, By *Howard Copenhaver, the latest collection of humorous ories. Contains rich humor and studied observations of a land Howard loves and the eople he met along the way in a lifetime spent in the wilds. 160 pages, many hotographs. Softcover only.*

hey Left Their Tracks, By *Howard Copenhaver, Recollections of Sixty Years as Wilderness Outfitter, 192 pages, clothbound or softcover editions (One of our all-me most popular books.)*

ore Tracks, By *Howard Copenhaver, 78 Years of Mountains, People & Happiness, 80 pages, clothbound or softcover editions.*

dian Trails & Grizzly Tales, By *Bud Cheff Sr., 212 pages, available in othbound and softcover editions.*

0,000 Miles Horseback In The Wilds of Idaho, By *Don Habel. Don Habel orked as an outfitter in the Idaho wilderness for more than forty years and has put gether a wonderfully detailed and sensitive, as well as occasionally humorous, minisce of his adventures in the wilds. 180 pages, softcover.*

ules & Mountains, By *Margie E. Hahn, the story of Walt Hahn, Forest Service acker, 164 pages, clothbound or softcover editions*

STONEYDALE PRESS PUBLISHING COMPANY

523 Main Street • Box 188
Stevensville, Montana 59870
Phone: 406-777-2729
Website: www.stoneydale.com